Praise for *Extraordinary PR, Ordinary Budget*

"When we worked together in the Forward Together Moral Monday movement, Jennifer Farmer skillfully heard me. She allowed me to be myself while highlighting for me and the North Carolina NAACP team foundational communications techniques."

—**Rev. Dr. William J. Barber, President, North Carolina State Conference of the NAACP, and architect of the Forward Together Moral Movement**

"Jennifer Farmer is one of the smartest and most talented communicators I know. She's passionate, knowledgeable, and relatable about her work. Plus, when we spent time together, she made sure I never ate alone."

—**Ari Berman, Contributing Writer, *The Nation***

"*Extraordinary PR, Ordinary Budget* is a practical and detailed guide for building and nurturing relationships with the media, relationships that will position your organization to make a lasting impact. This book is beyond helpful; it's necessary."

—**Judith Browne Dianis, Executive Director, Advancement Project National Office**

"The noise in the public square is deafening. And yet, more than ever, the ability to penetrate that noise so that your story can be heard is critical to successfully contesting for power. Jennifer defines a way to think and steps to take to insure your voice is heard. This book, filled with wisdom and practicality, is delivered with humor and passion."

—**Scott Reed, Executive Director, PICO National Network**

"I loved this book. It is smart, practical, and filled with personal examples that underscore the author's central message: there are concrete things you can do to promote your organization with or without a large budget. *Extraordinary PR, Ordinary Budget* is required reading for anyone wishing to use strategic communications to make a difference."

—**Celinda Lake, Principal, Lake Research Partners**

"*Extraordinary PR, Ordinary Budget* is one of those rare books that is straightforward and poignant. It guides readers in crafting an effective and executable PR strategy—all on a budget! This is required reading from a trusted PR expert!"

—**Becky Williams, President, SEIU 1199 WV/KY/OH**

· JENNIFER R. FARMER ·

EXTRAORDINARY
PR
ORDINARY
BUDGET

—— A Strategy Guide ——

BK

Berrett–Koehler Publishers, Inc.
a BK Business book

Berrett-Koehler Publishers, Inc.
1333 Broadway, Suite 1000 ▪ Oakland, CA 94612-1921
Tel: (510) 817-2277 ▪ Fax: (510) 817-2278 ▪ www.bkconnection.com

ORDERING INFORMATION

Quantity sales. Special discounts are available on quantity purchases by corporations, associations, and others. For details, contact the "Special Sales Department" at the Berrett-Koehler address above.

Individual sales. Berrett-Koehler publications are available through most bookstores. They can also be ordered directly from Berrett-Koehler: Tel: (800) 929-2929; Fax: (802) 864-7626; www.bkconnection.com

Orders for college textbook/course adoption use. Please contact Berrett-Koehler: Tel: (800) 929-2929; Fax: (802) 864-7626.

Orders by U.S. trade bookstores and wholesalers. Please contact Ingram Publisher Services, Tel: (800) 509-4887; Fax: (800) 838-1149; E-mail: customer.service@ ingrampublisherservices.com; or visit www.ingrampublisherservices.com/Ordering for details about electronic ordering.

Berrett-Koehler and the BK logo are registered trademarks of Berrett-Koehler Publishers, Inc.

Printed in the United States of America

Berrett-Koehler books are printed on long-lasting acid-free paper. When it is available, we choose paper that has been manufactured by environmentally responsible processes. These may include using trees grown in sustainable forests, incorporating recycled paper, minimizing chlorine in bleaching, or recycling the energy produced at the paper mill.

LIBRARY OF CONGRESS CATALOGING-IN-PUBLICATION DATA

Names: Farmer, Jennifer R., author.
Title: Extraordinary PR, ordinary budget : a strategy guide / Jennifer R. Farmer.
Description: First edition. | Oakland : Berrett-Koehler Publishers, [2017] | Includes bibliographical references and index.
Identifiers: LCCN 2017004121 | ISBN 9781626569935 (pbk. : alk. paper)
Subjects: LCSH: Public relations.
Classification: LCC HD59 .F334 2017 | DDC 659.2—dc23 LC record available at https://lccn.loc.gov/2017004121

FIRST EDITION

22 21 20 19 18 17 ▪ 10 9 8 7 6 5 4 3 2 1

Produced and designed by BookMatters, copyedited by Tanya Grove, proofed by Judy Loeven, indexed by Leonard Rosenbaum. Cover designed by Rob Johnson, Toprotype, Inc.

To my children
Cameron and Maya

CONTENTS

Preface *vii*

Introduction *xi*

ONE The Case for Communications 1

TWO Be Credible 17

THREE Be Creative 36

FOUR Be Responsive 53

FIVE Be Relentless 66

SIX Social Media on an Ordinary Budget 82

SEVEN PR Tactics on an Ordinary Budget 93

EIGHT Crisis Communications 126

Conclusion: Leading in the Midst of Fear
Using the Four Principles 137

Acknowledgments 147

Glossary 149

Notes 153

Index 158

About the Author 163

PREFACE

It is no coincidence that as the granddaughter of a pastor and the daughter of an evangelist—whose mission is to spread the gospel—I would enjoy a career as a communications professional. Just as an evangelist sees her work as spreading good news, my calling is to promote good causes that would otherwise go underappreciated. Just as an evangelist rails against sin, I rail against racial and social injustice. My passion for publicizing the work of organizations whose missions resonate with me could be compared to that of an evangelist on a God-directed mission.

I utilize every mode of communication (media relations, public relations, digital media, graphic design, training, events, etc.) to highlight injustice and urge accountability and change. When I'm traveling from city to city leading communications and media workshops for mission-driven organizations, I'm propelled by a passion to elevate work that would otherwise go unnoticed. The joy I feel upon placing a story about a pressing issue with a moral imperative in a national outlet, such as the *New York Times* or the *Washington Post*, or getting a guest column published in the opinion section of CNN.com or other well-respected media outlets is unrivaled. It is how I make an impact.

It should come as no surprise then that public relations and communications is a form of evangelism. I am not alone in this belief. Guy Kawasaki, former communications chief for Apple and author of more than thirteen books, considers himself an evangelist for the causes he passionately promotes.[1] Just like faith is a vehicle for some to achieve great things, I see communications as a tool to help organizations large and small achieve lofty and seemingly impossible goals.

The advice I offer here is drawn from personal experience. Over the course of my career, I have found myself at the center of major social justice movements and political campaigns. I did much of this work as a communications leader with a healthcare and social services union for the West Virginia, Kentucky, and Ohio region called Service Employees International Union District 1199 (WV/KY/OH), their international affiliate the Service Employees International Union (SEIU), and the national racial justice organization Advancement Project.

While serving on the international union staff for the SEIU, I spent time in Madison, Wisconsin, in 2011. I witnessed the height of major unrest before and after the passage of the then newly minted Governor Scott Walker's provision limiting collective bargaining for public sector unions.[2] I was part of a broader team of communications professionals flying into the state to provide assistance following a barrage of anti-union policies and proposals. I offered communication services such as crafting press releases, talking points, convening press events, and staffing high-level surrogates for public sector union members and leaders, including rank-and-file union member Ann Louise Tetreault, union leaders Bruce Colburn and Dian Palmer, and many others. I also had the pleasure of arranging media interviews for actor Tony Shalhoub who joined his sister, a teacher in Wisconsin's Denmark School System, in protesting the collective bargaining limitation.[3]

From 2004 to 2009, I worked on several political and issue-advocacy campaigns in Ohio while employed with the SEIU District 1199 (WV/KY/OH). The campaigns included a Paid Sick Days ballot initiative that would have kept working families from missing much-needed pay due to their illness or their child's illness. I also worked on a ballot initiative to defeat the Colorado-inspired Taxpayers Bill of Rights (TABOR), which would have shrunk government services by restricting revenue growth.

I've also worked on numerous political campaigns, including a brief stint on President Barack Obama's 2012 re-election campaign as communications director with Obama for America in Nevada, former Ohio Governor Ted Strickland's 2010 re-election campaign, and the 2004 and 2008 presidential campaigns as a member of the communications staff for SEIU District 1199 (WV/KY/OH).

My time on President Obama's 2012 re-election campaign was particularly memorable for the unrelenting nature of the work. My day started at 7 a.m., in time for a daily 7:30 a.m. conference call with communications directors and staff from western states, and usually ended around 10 p.m. Each week we plotted communications events, such as press conferences and other actions, with the goal of publicly defining the opponent, Mitt Romney, before he had an opportunity to define himself. Pulling off half a dozen press events per week was no small feat, but in the end it was incredibly effective as President Obama won the state of Nevada on election night.

These roles reinforced for me the importance of the four principles of extraordinary public relations: being credible, creative, responsive, and relentless. With more than fifteen years' experience working in communications and in the political and policy fields, I know firsthand the difference these four principles make. While the organizations I worked for had budgets of varying sizes, the key to success was always being credible, creative, responsive, and relentless. It was a surefire way to elevate issues that would otherwise go unnoticed or underappreciated.

Extraordinary PR, Ordinary Budget: A Strategy Guide is a natural by-product of my commitment to strengthen small organizations and grassroots campaigns by offering basic but critically important communications tips. This book is for the mission-driven organization that is spearheading critical work and seeking to promote its cause in the public domain. It is for the outfit that is doing everything right—yet few know they exist. It is for people who find themselves in a communications and public relations role for which they feel ill-equipped. It is for the grassroots leader seeking to elevate an organization's public profile. This manual is also for the executives and leaders looking to assess and evaluate his or her organization's communications program.

INTRODUCTION

Evangelism can be defined as spreading the gospel through personal witness and passionate advocacy. To be an effective evangelist, you must be passionately committed to your cause. But even unbridled passion is not enough. Being effective in anything, but especially communications and PR, requires creativity, credibility, responsiveness, and relentlessness.

In a twenty-four-hour news cycle with multiple issues competing for attention, it is imperative to understand how to break through in the media. It's not enough to build a vital, noteworthy campaign. If reporters don't find you *credible* (meaning they don't trust that you are an expert in your field or providing accurate information), if you aren't finding *creative* ways to garner attention, if you aren't *responsive* when the media reaches out or *relentless* when they don't, you're likely to experience minimal success.

Being Credible

You could have a public relations budget the size of Disney World, yet without credibility, members of the press will not take you seriously. What's more, once a PR professional or a spokesperson develops a reputation of lacking credibility, reporters may discount them as a source for future stories. It can make your organization a laughingstock in media newsrooms.

Most people don't set out to lack credibility. It happens when you, wittingly or not, provide inaccurate information that can damage your or a reporter's reputation. Imagine providing the wrong data to a journalist who includes it in her story. The journalists and the media outlet that employs them now run the risk of being forced to run a costly and embarrassing correction. Now, we're talking not only about damage to a reporter's reputation but also to their employer's.

Another way spokespeople get labeled untrustworthy is by being afraid to admit they don't know an answer when asked a question. Pretending to know the answer to a question is a surefire way to be labeled unreliable, and no amount of money in the world can solve credibility issues.

Being Creative

Money also doesn't correlate to creativity, which is the cornerstone of a winning pitch and sustained media attention. A pitch is a short paragraph or pithy statement explaining your issue and why it merits coverage or media interest. In media terms, creativity is about developing an unusual and appealing way to present information. It could be sharing information in the form of an infographic rather than a press release. It could be developing unusual props for a press conference.

The bottom line is that outside-the-box thinking is especially important when you work for a cash-strapped entity.

Reporters receive hundreds of press releases from competing interests, so thinking through creative and visually appealing ways to share information is key. If you're a one-person communications shop, you can network with other communicators from other organizations to get ideas for how to present information in unusual ways.

Being Responsive

By *responsive*, I mean replying to media inquiries in a timely fashion and using the initial contact as an opportunity to build a long-term relationship with a reporter. Responsiveness is about following through on promises to the media as well as to allies. It also means being prepared to jump on current events to tell a story you've been sitting on for months or longer.

Even if you're pressed for time and unable to provide a detailed response, a simple acknowledgment of a message shows a level of responsiveness that is appreciated by those working on tight deadlines. In fact, of all the work on my plate, I view media inquiries as one of the most important aspects of my job. That means I'll drop everything to research reporters (and their media outlets) who have contacted me for a story so I can respond effectively. I even make it a point to check my email a couple of times throughout the weekend so I can respond to after-hour inquiries as quickly as possible.

Being Relentless

To be relentless you must believe in something bigger than yourself. If you believe in something bigger than yourself, you'll go to the ends of the earth fighting for it.

Relentlessness is important in communications because public relations professionals are often bombarded with the word "no." It takes time and many rejections before successfully placing a news story. If you become discouraged after a reporter ignores or is disinterested in your pitch, you may be unwilling to pitch to other reporters. If this happens, you're likely to get minimal coverage. If you become discouraged when you don't get a timely response to a pitch and consequently fail to follow up, you might be missing an opportunity to engage a reporter who may simply be busy, rather than permanently uninterested in your story. Relentlessness is not shutting down at the first or second "no." It's also about refusing to believe a "no" today is a "no" tomorrow. Just because a reporter can't cover one story doesn't mean he or she will be unwilling to cover future stories. Moreover, a lack of an immediate response from a reporter could mean the reporter missed your email, and you may need to follow up. Maintaining enthusiasm in the face of "no" or in the face of silence is critical in this line of work.

How to Use This Book

While I've worked for organizations (such as SEIU and SEIU District 1199) who had paid media budgets, those budgets paled in comparison to those of corporations. I offer this information in the spirit of full disclosure, as even a modest paid media budget is more than what many of the people who read this book may enjoy.

Certainly, if you're working for a candidate for political office in an era of outsized money in politics and you're thinking about how to get your message out in the face of stiff opposition, you need significant funds. Imagine a presidential election in which one candidate had funds to advertise on television and the other did not; the person without the funds would surely lose. However, it's a little different if you work for a social impact entity. In this case, you do not need a multimillion-dollar communications budget (although I will not begrudge you if you have one) to elevate your organization's critical work. Your issues aren't less important because your budget is small. And regardless of your resources, the four principles to highlighting their importance remain the same: being relentless, responsive, credible, and creative. In drawing from my personal experience on a number of social justice campaigns, I provide a road map for using the four principles to successfully promote your issues—even on a cash-strapped budget.

In Chapter 1, I make the case for communications. When money is tight, spending it on communications can often seem superfluous. It is not. I explain why.

In Chapters 2 through 5, I dive deeply into each of the four principles. I use real-life examples to illustrate their power and provide concrete tips on how to leverage them to get the most bang for your buck. I also offer valuable no-cost tips for increasing your communication impact.

Chapter 6 is an exploration of how being credible, creative, responsive, and relentless apply to the growing and increasingly important area of social media PR.

Chapter 7 is full of hands-on budget-friendly PR tactics built on the foundation of the four principles.

Chapter 8 provides specific advice to communications professionals on how the four principles should come to the forefront when managing a crisis.

And last, I conclude with tips I learned along the way about how to press on in the midst of fear, burnout, failure, and doubt. The communications field can be very stressful yet rewarding. By applying the four principles I discuss in the book, maintaining a mind-set of reflection and growth, and finding aspects of your job that feed your spirit, you will undoubtedly find success.

My goal in writing this book is to provide a sound foundation for communications professionals who are struggling to make an impact on a limited organizational budget. My hope is that this book provides you not only with helpful tools to promote your issues in a cost-effective way but also with proof that if you stay on the track of being credible, creative, responsive, and relentless, you will have success. I did, and I hope my stories give you the resolve to keep on passionately evangelizing for worthy causes.

The Case for Communications

There's a reason press secretaries are among the first staff hired on political campaigns. The decision to appoint and train a team of communications professionals is among the most important actions a leader can take.

A well-trained communications team can challenge unjust or unpopular policy decisions, lay the groundwork for major public policy initiatives, catapult a professional career, influence the outcome of political campaigns, establish a favorable narrative or counteract a problematic one, and support or decimate a company's brand. For the organization or campaign, communications can mean the difference between success and failure.

Communications is a broad umbrella under which public relations, media relations—including paid and earned media—rapid response, digital media, graphic design, and print and production all fall. For the purposes of this book, I focus on the broad umbrella of communications with an emphasis on public relations and earned media. If you're a cash-strapped organization, earned media (i.e., media coverage you don't have to pay for) will be your best friend.

I also discuss how public relations supports communications. By *public relations* I am referring to a well-intentioned and deliberate strategy to communicate who you are and what you represent to donors, clients, constituents, or customers through the media and other public channels. PR is both proactive (e.g., outlining an affirmative vision for an organization or leader) and reactive (e.g., responding to inquiries from any range of public outlets, including the media).

As essential as communications is to an organization, communicators and PR professionals sometimes get a bad rap. We are sometimes referred to as talking heads and accused of indiscriminately carrying our organization's water. While problematic, this is probably preferred to another common label: spin doctors. These are, of course, pessimistic views of communications and public relations. But keep in mind that my brand of public relations is mission-driven, communications for organizations whose sole objective is making the world a better place. There is nothing wrong with advocating on behalf of a mission-driven organization or an issue you truly believe in. And there is nothing undesirable about advocating on behalf of groups working to address pressing societal issues, such as structural racism, social injustice, inequities in education, income inequality, and poverty.

Communications for Mission-Driven Organizations

For the mission-driven organization, communications is a powerful tool to rail against injustice. If you don't like the way politicians treat the least of us, there are myriad communications tactics—such as showcasing testimonials from impacted communities through a photo series or YouTube videos, highlighting the impact of a proposed policy through an infographic, an open letter shared with the press, media conference calls, newspaper ads, and video press releases—to publicize the impact of public policy and encourage decision-makers to reverse course.

When combating unjust policies, a well-oiled communications and public relations program can allow a mission-driven organization to punch above its weight class. I learned this firsthand as a communications staffer for the local healthcare and social services union SEIU District 1199 (WV/KY/OH). Union representatives were negotiating a collective bargaining agreement for nursing-home workers in West Virginia. As you can imagine, most nursing-home workers (who are at the heart of the nursing-home industry) make very little money, even as they sometimes pay exorbitant fees for necessities such as healthcare insurance. At the same time, nursing-home owners enjoy much higher salaries and profit margins than the frontline staff who allow the business to thrive. Like everyone else, nursing-home workers want to be able to care for their patients and earn enough money to support their families. In this case, winning in the court of public opinion required us to present a stark contrast between perceived right and wrong. We had to highlight the discrepancy between the salaries and profit margins of nursing-home owners and operators and that of their staff. Painting a clear picture of how nursing-home workers are suffering in the face of these disparities was the key to invoking demand for change.

Consider also the digital advocacy group Color of Change, led by Rashad Robinson.[1] Color of Change has launched a series of powerful campaigns that have held multimillion-dollar corporations accountable to local communities. They played a key role in exposing the American Legislative Exchange Council (ALEC) and what some would characterize as ALEC's nefarious policies to push template legislation that is harmful to working families and communities of color in state legislatures across the country. ALEC is a membership-based organization that spends significant sums of money lavishing expensive trips on lawmakers who are then encouraged to introduce model legislation advancing conservative ideology in their respective state legislatures. The policies include anti-voting measures and stand-your-ground laws that have a disparate impact on communities of color. In addition, ALEC's policies have adversely impacted working-class individuals and families, drawing the ire of labor unions and left-leaning political groups.

Color of Change launched petitions, sent direct mailers to companies that were members of ALEC, regularly sent email updates to their hundreds of thousands of followers, and generally called out ALEC using every traditional and social media platform available. The emails directed followers to take action that in turn placed pressure on the companies that were members of ALEC. The campaign succeeded in causing grave embarrassment for dozens of companies, which led many to part ways with ALEC as the *National Journal* reported on November 10, 2014:

ALEC has witnessed a torrent of high-profile departures in the past. In 2012, a collection of major corporations, including Blue Cross Blue Shield, Coca-Cola, PepsiCo, and Kraft, left the organization following public outcry over the group's then-sponsorship of controversial "Stand Your Ground" laws, which came under heavy scrutiny during the Trayvon Martin case. The organization no longer works on legislation related to firearms.[2]

While there were many groups, including labor unions and legislative watchdogs, who launched accountability campaigns targeting ALEC, the role of Color of Change cannot be understated in successfully calling out the organization and bringing about positive change. There's another, more practical reason for highlighting the Color of Change ALEC campaign. It is an example of what can be accomplished when groups with similar ideologies work together.

Working in tandem with other groups on a specific campaign is a key strategy for maximizing limited resources. In the civil rights community, organizations that challenge barriers to voting, such as The Leadership Conference on Civil and Human Rights, NYU's Brennan Center for Justice, the NAACP Legal Defense Fund, and Advancement Project, often work collaboratively. When one organization is leading litigation or the work around a specific case, other organizations routinely offer aid—even if that aid is limited to helping to promote the case or frame it in the proper context in the media. Through regular calls for communicators, lawyers, and other civil rights advocates, work is easily divided up, and individual players get more accomplished. For instance, when Advancement Project was preparing for a legal appeal to North Carolina's anti-voting measure, I organized numerous conference calls with voting rights advocates and communicators in which I outlined communications needs and asked different coalition members to help fulfill those needs. During the calls, I requested groups issue press releases, write opinion essays, and assist with promotion of the case on social media. Many obliged my request.

Advancement Project reaped many victories using aggressive communications campaigns during my time there. In 2013, my former colleague Cynthia Gordy organized a media conference call for our partner New Florida Majority, sent a powerful press release, and drafted a compelling opinion piece questioning an amendment to Florida's omnibus budget bill (Senate Bill 600). The measure would have required voters with disabilities, persons with limited literacy, and those with language barriers to personally know their assistors prior to receiving help on Election Day. The amendment would have also restricted assistors to helping ten people each. Many felt the measure was put forward to make it harder for certain voters, namely those who vote Democratic, to cast a ballot. Following immense public pressure that included nonstop media coverage featuring the people most impacted by the measure, the sponsor of the amendment, Senator Jack Latvala, pulled the proposal from consideration in 2013.[3] Had we passively allowed the debate to play out solely in the halls of the legislature without the glare of media scrutiny, the harmful and unnecessary measure would likely have gone into effect.

One more example: In the spring of 2013, the Reverend Dr. William J. Barber II of the North Carolina State Conference of the National Association for the Advancement of Colored People (NC NAACP) organized "Moral Monday" protests at the North Carolina General Assembly. Barber's Moral Monday protests were one part of his broader Forward Together movement, which advocated fusion or coalition politics, the likes of which had not been seen since the civil rights movement of the 1950s and '60s. Barber was at the helm of not only the NC NAACP but also the Historic Thousands on Jones Street People's Assembly Coalition, and serves as senior pastor of Greenleaf Christian Church in Goldsboro, North Carolina. He is accomplishing in North Carolina what many political parties in states across the country have been unable to do: challenge unjust policies through the lens of morality, hold political leaders accountable, and build cross-cultural and ecumenical alliances.

His weekly protests challenged a wave of extreme and regressive policies passed by ultra-conservatives in the state legislature. At the conclusion of the first wave of Moral Monday protests in 2013 and 2014, close to a thousand people had been arrested for peacefully petitioning their elected leaders for a redress of grievances. The protesters included doctors, nurses, teachers, and students. They entered the statehouse to pray, sing, and meet with their legislators but were charged with trespassing and disturbing the peace. Media coverage of the protests and arrests gave Rev. Barber and his colleagues the opportunity to reach a much broader audience with powerful moral messages about the immoral and illegitimate laws being passed by the General Assembly.

While the concerned community leaders never should have been arrested and charged in the first place, the sustained organizing work and the help of over 100 volunteer lawyers who defended the protesters, created an environment where charges against hundreds of people were ultimately dropped. They did this by being in constant contact with the community and highlighting the immoral policies being passed by the legislature. This allowed the community to understand what was at stake and support the resistance movement. Additionally, the contact with the community was covered favorably in the press, which kept the momentum on the side of the organizers. It was the massive grassroots movement afoot in North Carolina led by Rev. Dr. Barber and the people participating in the Moral Monday protests that laid the groundwork for the dismissal of charges.[4]

I should mention that the goal of Barber's movement was not primarily to get the charges dismissed but rather to get the North Carolina legislature to change course.

Communicating Your Alpha Dog Story

The organizations that stand out and have the most trusted brands have at least one thing in common: a strong communications infrastructure. Note I wrote "strong" not "costly." While considerable resources are needed for political campaigns, organizations can get by with far smaller communications budgets. So long as communications team members are credible, creative, responsive, and relentless, they can work miracles in terms of their ability to effectively advocate on the organization's behalf. As I explore throughout this book, communicators can use these four principles to create an effective narrative or Alpha Dog story about their organizations regardless of their budgets. They can also use these principles to change an unhelpful Alpha Dog story that may have been created prior to the communicator joining an organization.

The Alpha Dog story is one of the earliest and most defining stories written or produced about your organization, candidate, or campaign. The person or entity who creates the story benefits from defining an organization or campaign before others have an opportunity to do so. Former *USA Today* reporter and author Sally Stewart, describes the Alpha Dog frame this way:

> When an editor assigns a story about a company to a reporter, the first move the reporter makes is to seek out everything that has ever been written about that company. The Internet has made that process very easy. At some of the larger newspapers, magazines, and TV news shows, the reporter calls the in-house librarian and orders a Lexis-Nexis search. If the resulting research turns up unflattering facts, such as a pattern of unscrupulous business practices and faulty merchandise, it's a given that the reporter will mention those old accusations in her new story. Moreover, it doesn't matter if the company has changed or if new management is in charge. The first story written about the company is the Alpha Dog Story, and the Alpha Dog leads the pack. Therefore, it is absolutely essential to any company that you take time securing that all-important Alpha Dog Story, as it will determine your company's coverage for years to come.[5]

If the Alpha Dog story is negative or unflattering, as Stewart mentions, you and your organization are invariably and unceremoniously on the defense. The defense is obviously the unwanted position in politics, business, and grassroots organizing because it surrenders control. Rather than pushing your message, you are spending your time responding to a set of questions and circumstances that you did not create. You are in a reactive versus proactive position.

In politics, it is often said that arguing on an opponent's frame is a losing proposition. What does this mean? If I set the frame, I am crafting it in a way that is beneficial to me and the issue I'm advocating. My opponents who engage on my terms, using my frame, are at a distinct disadvantage. What is more, an unhelpful Alpha Dog narrative lingers like a bad cold or a house guest who has long overstayed his welcome.

I've had several experiences challenging harmful Alpha Dog stories. When I joined the labor union SEIU District 1199 (WV/KY/OH) in August 2004 as a communications coordinator, I was thrilled to be leading communications and advocacy work for an organization representing nursing homes, hospitals, libraries, Head Start facilities, and public sector employees. The work was not without its challenges. For decades, there has been an intense backlash against labor unions. In 1945, more than a third of working people belonged to unions.[6] In 1998, just 13.9 percent of people belonged to unions. Today, the percentage of union membership in the private sector is in the single digits. Since fewer people belong to unions, fewer people understand the role labor unions play—and have played—in our society. Moreover, decreased membership also means unions lack the power they had in earlier eras. Since opposition to their existence is fierce, highlighting working conditions for working-class people through earned media was beyond difficult. The court of public opinion was not on our side, and many reporters often seemed hostile to our pitches. The only exception was when the spokesperson was a rank-and-file union member (as opposed to a paid union staff member or leader). When we did score press coverage, such as news articles and editorials, I noticed they were laced with personal jabs at our then president, Dave Regan.

The bad blood stemmed in part from the union's position on a 2003 ballot measure that levied a special tax on Cuyahoga County homeowners to pay for services for indigent families and persons with disabilities. In exchange for supporting the levy, the union asked county officials to commit to refraining from using public funds to launch high-pressure, anti-union campaigns. When the county refused to do so, the union launched a campaign urging defeat of the levy. This approach backfired horribly. Asking the public to defeat a levy for persons with disabilities—who serve as wonderful messengers and automatically garner public sympathy—was a losing proposition. Trying to explain to the public what happens when companies run anti-union campaigns also proved difficult in an environment where union membership was particularly low. The union was fighting a losing battle, and the media ruthlessly attacked us and our leader, Dave Regan. Our unwanted Alpha Dog story was that we were bullies who didn't care about people with disabilities.

The media turned every mention of our organization into an opportunity to remind readers of our earlier opposition to the levy and the attacks went on for over a year. We eventually hired a savvy media consultant, Dale Butland, who developed a plan to allow the union to move from defense to offense. Butland's plan included a statewide editorial board tour permitting Regan to explain who he was and his vision for making life easier for working people, such as nurses, prison psychiatrists, Head Start workers, home health aides, and librarians. It was only after we crisscrossed the state meeting with editorial boards large and small that the vilification in the press finally subsided.

The editorial board meetings allowed us to humanize Regan. It allowed him an opportunity to display his concern for working families, including union and nonunion households. Regan is an Ivy League–educated leader, so he also challenged preconceived notions about so-called union bosses. There wasn't a question he was asked during the editorial boards that he couldn't answer. After the meetings, most editorial boards had an understanding, if not appreciation, for Regan and the work he was spearheading.

It bears mentioning that leadership matters. If the media is impressed with your organization's leader and mission, it's easier to garner favorable news coverage. If donors and investors have confidence in an institution's leader, they are more likely to invest financial resources in the entity. Let this serve as a reminder to leaders who do everything in their power to avoid the media: reporters cannot get to know you if you avoid them. Preserving or repairing a leader's image is imperative to an organization. Failure to do so may result in the furtherance of an unhelpful Alpha Dog story, which can follow an organization or company for years. A bad Alpha Dog story is more than a temporary inconvenience or black eye. It casts aspersions and results in costly distractions from the important work your organization is doing.

A strong public relations program can help create a positive Alpha Dog story so that the organization can focus on the issues that really matter. And developing a strong program is as simple as being creative, credible, responsive, and relentless.

Your Seat at the Table

The most important point to keep in mind about using communications to further your organization's goals is that the communications team must be fully integrated in all strategic discussions. This allows communicators to understand the thinking behind different proposals and craft plans to support various organizational campaigns. This integration must happen early and often. Here's why: The communications field is broader than mere implementation. It also involves thinking strategically about the impact of various business decisions and outlining best practices for how to talk about those decisions. "Communicators," as my former boss Dave Regan would chide, "aren't maintenance repairmen." We don't exist to fulfill orders, and forcing us to carry out someone else's vision without an opportunity to co-develop work plans is ineffective and demoralizing. The integration of communications should be substantive, meaning the communications and PR team must have a say in the development and execution of strategic decisions. When you combine the perspective and input of public relations professionals with a carefully crafted strategic plan, you help maximize output and ensure the very best outcomes for your issue-advocacy campaign or organization. You also ensure your communications team feels valued and respected, which can help with retention. Organizations get a bigger bang for their buck if communicators are included at the outset of the campaign.

Communicators: The key to making the case for inclusion at the outset of campaigns is persistence. Be relentless in making the case for your inclusion in the early phases of campaigns. Frame your argument in a way that shows how your early involvement benefits your manager and organization. For example, "You'll understand the strategy, which will prepare you to develop appropriate communications plans and tactics." People are ultimately self-interested; so appeal to something they want, and you'll set yourself up for success.

Executives: It is costly and distracting to constantly replace staff, including communicators. Involving them in the early phases of a campaign boosts morale while ensuring you are benefitting from diverse perspectives. Early engagement of your communications team also gives them an opportunity to develop communications plans to carry out your work while also nurturing relationships with the media. If your staff members appreciate a heads-up on important projects, imagine how overworked journalists feel.

In the end, early involvement of communicators benefits both communicators and the organizations they serve.

Tactics versus Principles

Now that we're clear on the important role of communications in furthering your organization's goals, I will dissect the four principles of extraordinary communications as they apply to issue-advocacy campaigns and mission-driven organizations. When thinking about the elements for success in public relations, you may be tempted to focus solely on specific tactics. I am resisting this urge since I believe the four principles of being credible, creative, responsive, and relentless are as big a determinant to success as tactics. If you indiscriminately employ tactics without following core standards, your success may be short-lived or inconsistent at best. But if you operate from a blueprint that outlines the importance of, for example, responsiveness to a deadline-driven media, you'll be far more effective than focusing on the tactic of, say, sending a press release.

Moreover, tactics can and should vary from campaign to campaign and from organization to organization. They are influenced by a variety of factors including organizational culture and long-term campaign goals. I cannot possibly advise you on a comprehensive set of tactics to promote your issue or cause without a deeper understanding of the organizational culture and, more important, the goals of a given campaign. If the goal is to pressure an employer to allow workers to have a voice on the job and bargain collectively, the communications tactics may be far more aggressive than if the goal is to applaud an institution for implementing a favorable policy. But regardless of the tactic, principles matter. So, while I do highlight a range of tactics throughout the book (and particularly in Chapter 7), I invest more time in principles. My promise: if you follow the principles outlined in the next four chapters, you will be much better prepared to successfully implement the tactics your institutions and internal leadership team shape.

Be Credible

One of the earliest lessons I learned as a communicator was the importance of credibility. I was working for the then 30,000-member SEIU District 1199 (WV/KY/OH) as a communications coordinator. It was my first job at a labor union, and I knew very little about the labor movement. I'd always considered myself an advocate for marginalized communities, so leading communications for a labor union seemed like a natural fit. Furthermore, I was committed to learning as much as I possibly could. What I lacked in technical skill was compensated by a desire to learn.

As I mentioned earlier, the union's then president, David Regan, hired communications consultant Dale Butland to add capacity to our communications efforts and to help me further develop my communications skillset. Butland was once press secretary for the late Ohio senator, John Glenn. He was also the first communications consultant I worked with. I would later learn that working with consultants is commonplace for many communicators. As such, learning to work effectively with consultants is critical to a communicator's success.

During that early relationship with Butland, I learned the benefit of asking questions rather than relying on him to do those things I didn't know how to do. I would watch him and try to learn by observation. My boss supported this approach as well.

Rather than relegate me to a behind-the-scenes role, Dave and one of his then vice presidents, Becky Williams (who was elected president of the union in 2008), instructed Butland to teach me everything from requesting and then participating in editorial board meetings to staying calm in the face of a crisis to thinking creatively about ways to generate media coverage.

Perhaps the most enduring lesson Butland shared was when he came into my office to discuss strategies for building mutually beneficial relationships with journalists. In a very serious tone, he told me if I didn't maintain credibility with reporters, I would be no good to the organization or the press. I would be useless.

As someone who cared deeply about the union members we represented, the thought of alienating the media and potentially being unable to tell the stories of working families was unbearable. I was desperate to please; the last thing I wanted to do was develop a reputation of being untrustworthy.

I quickly learned that being credible is about knowing which stories are newsworthy and which stories are not. One way to earn the unenviable title of novice is to develop a pattern of pitching stories that are of little news value. A critical point to remember is that credible public relations professionals can spot the difference between a story that is newsworthy and one that is not.

For the spokesperson or public relations staffer, being credible is also about being informed. This means having a baseline understanding of the reporters who cover the beats of interest to you as well as the more technical information about the issue you're pitching. Last, credibility is about being recognized for following through on your word: doing what you said you would do and not doing what you said you wouldn't. It's about being honest.

Communicators working for organizations with limited means: You will be happy to learn that being credible is one of the easiest communications principles to follow on a budget. It literally costs nothing. Keeping your word, knowing what's newsworthy, and being informed don't take anything more than your time and your integrity.

Keep Your Word

Obviously, as communicators, your word matters. Think about the oft-used technique known as the "embargo," which is an agreement to share information with the media with the understanding that it will be shared publicly only after an agreed-upon date. Before many entities release reports, they often share a preview copy with trusted reporters under an agreement that the reporter will not report on the material before the embargo is lifted. Both the reporter and the public relations professional are expected to abide by the embargo.

Embargoes allow reporters to prepare their stories in advance of a major announcement or prior to the release of a report. Then, once the announcement is made, they can quickly publish their already-written stories on the topic.

I learned the hard way how not being clear on the terms of an embargo agreement can damage credibility. I was working for Advancement Project and was serving as communications lead on a campaign to combat overly harsh school disciplinary policies. I was pulled in at the behest of the parent and youth group Padres y Jovenes Unidos to promote a historic intergovernmental agreement between Denver Public Schools and the Denver Police Department that stipulated and limited the role of police in schools. The agreement held promise for reducing racial disparities in school discipline and reducing out-of-school suspensions. This was important because racial disparities in discipline and out-of-school suspensions decrease instruction time and increase the likelihood a student will drop out of high school altogether. In 2013, the Civil Rights Project's Center for Civil Rights Remedies at UCLA found that "reserving out-of-school suspension as a measure of last resort can lead to higher achievement and improved graduation rates."[1]

The agreement had all the trappings of a good story—unique, timely, and counterintuitive (a police department working with a community group)—and I wanted to secure national media coverage. In mapping my strategy, I opted to place the story with a national media outlet, one influential enough that if they covered it, other papers would follow suit.

I decided to pitch the story and give first right of refusal to the *Washington Post*. The *Post*, in turn, decided to run the story on the condition I give it to them as an exclusive, meaning they would be the first to break the news of the agreement. Always ambitious, I continued to pitch the story but created an embargo for other media outlets. However, I wasn't transparent with them. I didn't tell them the *Washington Post* would be covering the agreement as an exclusive and that their stories would run a full day after the *Post* story ran. What a rookie mistake!

Think about the position this left the education beat reporters at the other media outlets. Some likely faced pressure from their editors who demanded to know why the *Washington Post* broke the story rather than them. I will never forget the call I received from reporter Nirvi Shah from *Education Week*, the industry paper for education (Shah now works for POLITICO). I had taken a day off from work and was visiting family when I received the call from Shah. The woman whom I had known as only friendly and warm called in a fury. She wanted to know why I made the decision to give the story to the *Washington Post* as opposed to *Education Week* and why I didn't tell her I had done so. She was highly upset and rightly so. I listened patiently to what felt like a never-ending phone call. I begged Shah not only for her forgiveness but for the opportunity to make it right. She was not easily appeased. I hung up the phone and began thinking about my options for getting back in her good graces and regaining my credibility.

First, I arranged a one on one between Shah and my boss

at the time, Advancement Project's Judith Browne Dianis, who was a pioneer in the movement to end overly harsh school disciplinary policies. To make it worth Shah's time, I knew Browne Dianis would need to provide as-yet-to-be disclosed information on one of our campaigns. I remembered my organization hosted a two-day gathering of more than a hundred youth from across the country for an Action Camp, a space to allow young people to think through strategies for ending the school-to-prison pipeline and improving school culture. The school-to-prison pipeline is the patchwork of overly harsh school disciplinary policies and practices that funnel children (especially children of color, children with disabilities, and students identifying as LGBT) from the classroom to the criminal justice system. The gatherings were typically private sessions and not open to press. However, my relationship with Shah and *Education Week* was worth a departure from the rules. I got permission for Shah not only to join us but also to have access to all workshops and panels. When I presented the idea to Shah, I also promised her that I would identify youth who would speak with her and share their stories. The plan went perfectly.

Shah was the first reporter we welcomed into an Action Camp space, and she was the only reporter at the 2013 camp. In the end, I restored my relationship with her, scoring a front-page story in *Education Week* in the process. I was extremely lucky. Following my foray into disaster, I became determined to be more careful and forthright so as not to damage relationships with reporters or compromise my credibility. Use my experience as a cautionary tale!

Know What's Newsworthy

When seeking to promote your campaign or organization, look for elements of your work that are unusual, interesting, and unique. These are the elements that reporters use to determine what will be covered.

The media is not interested in telling a story that is uninteresting, essentially a story that won't appeal to their audiences. And as remarkable as the PR skillset can be, communicators are not magicians. We cannot magically make a story appear in print. An issue either has the trappings of a good story or it does not.

A good story begs to be covered. It includes items that provoke a second read or double-take or that inspire. Examples of good stories include those that coincide with current events, those that highlight a compelling personal narrative, and those that are counterintuitive. It compels you upon reading just the headline to want to know more. It answers the question "Why should I care?"

While the importance of having a newsworthy story is simple enough in theory, it's sometimes difficult to explain to non-communications professionals. Just because an issue is important internally doesn't make it a good news story. Anyone who's worked in communications for any length of time has been on the receiving end of a non-communications staff person claiming to have an issue that should be on the front page of your local or state paper. Similarly, most reporters, editors, or producers have been on the receiving end of a communications or public relations professional seeking in vain to convince them to cover something that isn't appealing. Just because you care doesn't mean the public will.

So how should communications staff respond when they've been ordered to generate media coverage for an issue? You respond by acknowledging your concerns and explaining to coworkers and higher-ups what constitutes a good story. Explain the other issues presently in the news cycle that may affect media coverage. Sort through the details of an issue to find the most compelling lede or angle and then use that in your pitch. The most important thing is helping your peers understand that communicators must answer the "Why should I care?" question for the media.

The "Why should I care?" answer isn't always obvious. It sometimes takes a bit of creativity to find (See Chapter 3). But sometimes a newsworthy story just falls into your lap, like this one: honor student, Kiera Wilmot, whom I had the pleasure of working with for several years, was arrested, expelled, and charged with two felonies for a science project gone wrong. In essence, she was expelled because of a passion for science. How's that for a lede?

Kiera created a makeshift volcano that did what it was designed to do: erupt. She proudly took it to school to show her teachers and peers. But instead of accolades for her accomplishment, what she got was handcuffs and an arrest record. Though no one was hurt and there was no property damage, the standout student was sent to the principal's office and put on a path to academic ruin.

Kiera's story seems counterintuitive. We don't typically

think of honor students being in trouble, much less expelled and arrested. So that piece of information alone immediately caught reporters' attention. It was a story that naturally provoked curiosity and interest. If an honor student can be arrested and charged with felonies, what can we expect for other children?

Kiera's experience presented an opportunity to highlight for reporters the challenges with overly harsh school disciplinary policies and practices as well as disparities in school discipline. Her experience also helped to illustrate the challenges with police in schools.

After hearing of this young girl's experience, I was naturally heartbroken. I'm a mother and empathized with Kiera and her family. Sensing in her story a window to talk about school discipline, an issue that doesn't always get the attention it deserves, I reached out to Kiera and her mother to ask their permission in helping to share their story with the world. They agreed and a partnership ensued. I convinced my employer, Advancement Project, to feature Kiera in an animated video on the dangers of police in schools and harsh school disciplinary policies and practices.[2] Within twenty-four hours of posting the video, it garnered thousands of views on YouTube, Facebook, and Twitter.

I had previously spent months focused on publicizing the problems with the school-to-prison pipeline and overly harsh school discipline. Here was an opportunity to make real the anecdotes I had been peddling to education reporters. Now while the video was part of a much larger and higher-budgeted campaign, Kiera's inclusion didn't cost an extra cent. All it took was a well-honed sense that her story was counterintuitive and would appeal to reporters.

During this process, I learned another important lesson. Sometimes the timing of a story may make it less newsworthy. When we finished the video, I didn't have a news hook or a reason for releasing it. It didn't correspond to items in the news cycle; it wasn't timely. I knew it was a good video and would capture media attention if released at an opportune moment. As such, I held it. When Kiera's mother contacted me several months later to tell me Kiera would indeed graduate from high school, I knew my moment had come. Connecting the release of the video to Kiera's graduation created a timely news hook—reporters were already preparing graduation stories—and increased the likelihood that the media would report on Kiera's ordeal.

Even if you have the makings of a great story, current events may decrease the likelihood of your issue being covered. Think of the major events and themes that have dominated national headlines recently: the Sony hack, countless police shootings of unarmed African American men and boys, ISIS and other threats to national security, the Ebola and Zika outbreaks, and the 2016 presidential election. If you pitched a story to national or even local news on the day these or other major issues broke and your story was unrelated to these headlines, your coverage was likely adversely impacted. It's very possible that you pitched a newsworthy item, and perhaps under a different set of circumstances or at a different time, you may have received better coverage.

Again, each story you pitch should be tied to a specific news hook or an item that makes it relevant. For instance, pitching a story on famed civil rights leader Fannie Lou Hamer may be pointless if the story isn't pegged to the anniversary of an important event, such as Freedom Summer, of which she was a part; the birth of the Mississippi Freedom Democratic Party, for which she served in a leadership role; her birth; or her death. As enduring a civil rights leader as Hamer may be, you are unlikely to place an article about her out of the blue. Regardless of how talented a public relations professional you may be, there is only so much you can do without a legitimate news hook.

To capture a reporter's interest and increase the likelihood of coverage, answer the following questions:

- Why is this story important now?

- What makes your story or angle unique?

- Why should anyone care?

- Would the story be more appealing to one media outlet versus another?

- Is the issue you're pitching the first of its kind?

- Is the issue you're pitching the largest or most comprehensive sort of policy?

Remember, the goal of all of this is maintaining your credibility so you can effectively promote your organization's issues and campaigns in the future. You want members of the press to take you seriously. You do not want to develop a reputation for continually pitching non-news stories because that would lead to a lack in your credibility. When you reach out to members of the media, try to be as objective as possible. If you were not affiliated with the organization in question, would you care or want to know about the news item the group is pitching or promoting? If you had to decide between this and other issues, would this one stand out? And if you think you're unable to be objective, ask a friend or family member whether they think the issue is interesting. If it passes the test and they express interest, you may be on the right track.

Be Informed

Prior to meeting with members of the media—reporters, producers, TV hosts, and others—learn as much as you can about the person or entity with whom you are meeting. This will ensure you're reaching out to the appropriate person and will help you avoid the embarrassment that inevitably comes with being ill-informed. Before you ever get a reporter on the phone or meet with a reporter or producer, you should have a sense of the issues they cover, the media outlets they currently and previously worked for, and maybe their general topics of interest.

If I want to reach a journalist, especially someone with whom I've seldom or never worked, I will use every method (email, phone, direct message, etc.) at my disposal to contact them. Once I've interacted with a reporter (i.e., they've answered an email or phone call or I've provided sources for a story they've written), I have a sense of whether they prefer to be contacted by email, phone, or, in rare instances, via a digital media platform. Many journalists will tell you right away they favor email rather than phone pitches. This is understandable. There's nothing more frustrating than being "in the zone" and getting interrupted by an unsolicited phone call. In cases where I know a journalist prefers email pitches, I will send the pitch via email. If I don't receive a response in a couple days, I'll follow up with another email. In rare circumstances, if I need an immediate response, I may leave a voicemail message. If I know the journalist prefers email pitches, I will do my best to respect their wishes, using voicemail only as a last resort. There are a few exceptions. Some reporters take several days to follow up on email inquiries. If the reporter is someone with whom I have a relationship and I know the person takes a day or so to get back to me, I will wait for a response. I just plan my pitch accordingly, building in enough time for their anticipated response.

In addition to understanding the preferred method of contact, it's also important to have a sense of the best time to reach members of the media. I occasionally pitch *New York Times* education editor Motoko Rich. After pitching various items, I learned I will always get a response, but those responses will usually come early in the morning— before a hectic schedule and the rush to meet deadlines absorb much of her day. As such, I try to send Rich emails before 8 a.m., ideally before her inbox is filled with myriad other pitches and solicitations.

Understanding the best time to reach members of the media also includes a sense of their work schedules. Some

TV producers who work on shows that air on the weekends, like MSNBC's AM Joy, are off a couple days during the week since they work on Saturdays and Sundays. Some print journalists, such as *USA Today* reporters, are off one day during the week. If you're pitching a journalist from this outlet about a media conference call on a Monday, you'll need to begin pitching them on Wednesday or Thursday, since they're off Fridays. Be sure to research the work schedules for the reporters you intend to pitch.

Once you have a grasp of the work schedule, have narrowed down the preferred method to reach the reporter, and know the best time of day to phone or email, gather research on the journalist's background and the subject areas they cover. You also want to have a sense of the types of stories the journalist has recently covered. This can be found via a simple Google search of the person's name.

Collecting as much information on members of the media as possible is important for several reasons. First, if you plan to pitch a reporter on a police brutality or voting rights story, for example, you should know if they or their media outlet is amenable to such a topic. In other words, does the topic fit or appeal to their audience? Also, is it a topic they've covered recently? There's no sense pitching a reporter on a topic or story they've recently written about unless you have substantive information that would make a follow-up story appealing; and by "substantive," I mean groundbreaking. Here's a hypothetical situation where a follow-up might be in order. In November 2013, Broward County Public Schools, the Fort Lauderdale Police Department, and other municipal and community-based entities (such as the Fort Lauderdale/ Broward County Branch of the NAACP) signed a collaborative agreement on school discipline. The agreement limited out-of-school suspensions, school-based arrests, and harsh school disciplinary policies as a step toward dismantling the school-to-prison pipeline. The story received widespread attention in state and national media.

When I pitched the *Washington Post* about covering the agreement, they declined, as they had already covered a similar agreement in Denver, the one I had pitched earlier in the year. It would have taken the hand of God descending from the sky to make the *Washington Post* reconsider. However, the paper may have done a follow-up had it been discovered that Broward County Public Schools officials offered kickbacks to the local police department as a condition for getting them to sign the agreement. This is patently false, of course; but if it were true, it would have led to a follow-up story. If one or two years later, school-based arrests and out-of-school suspensions had decreased significantly and resulted in improved academic outcomes, that also could have prompted a follow-up.

While these are examples of the basic criteria for follow-up stories, the broader point is that without conducting a recent review of articles, you may miss critical information and waste your, as well as the journalist's, time. Moreover, making these mistakes could damage your credibility. There are few things as embarrassing as enthusiastically sharing what you think is a new story idea or concept only to have the journalist tell you they or their outlet recently covered it. This sort of faux pas, especially if it happens repeatedly, makes you look uninformed. It's an error anyone in communications for any length of time has made and one we hope others will not repeat. Certainly, we all make mistakes, but doing your research will ensure you do not develop a pattern of being uninformed.

Pardon me if I'm stating the obvious, but if you're going to send an email pitch or phone a reporter, you'll want to have the best contact information for the reporter or producer. When I say "best" I mean the contact information that the reporter, editor, or producer regularly checks. In some cases, the best contact information may be a personal email address or a cell phone number. I was following up with an opinion editor at CNN.com, Pat Wiedenkeller, urging her to give me a decision on a piece I'd recently submitted. I learned from experience the best way to reach Wiedenkeller was on her cell phone. I phoned just after 8 a.m. and she hurriedly answered the phone. My excitement upon hearing Wiedenkeller's voice rather than a voicemail dissipated within seconds as she rushed me off the phone. The call was unusually abrupt. As it turns out I'd reached Wiedenkeller on her home phone just as she was rushing out the door to get to the office. She'd previously left messages from the phone number in question and being the diligent contact-collecting PR professional I am, I expeditiously locked the number into my contacts. Oh, the horror to have Wiedenkeller tell me I had reached her at her home. I apologized and promptly marked the number as her home number. Notice I didn't delete it. This would prevent me from making the same mistake again and unnecessarily ruffling her feathers. Again, get a sense of the best number or email to reach your media contacts and then ensure you're using the correct one.

Additionally, newsrooms are rapidly evolving with journalists often transitioning from one media outlet to another. To ensure you continue to have the best information for members of the media, you'll want to constantly (monthly if possible) update your media lists and contacts. Among other options, you can do this by reviewing the bounce-backs on emails.

Maintaining accurate contact information is critical as this will enable you to expeditiously respond in a crisis or rapid-response situation. While this sounds like a full-time job, there are resources, such as Crystal Knows, Dylan Byers' media blog for CNN (he once did this for POLITICO), and POLITICO New York, that help public relations professionals and others stay on top of transitions at various media outlets. Crystal Knows also helps members learn the preferred communication styles of media and online personalities, helping to ensure your pitch makes an impact and sees results. The Huffington Post also has a media page that is filled with helpful information about the national media. It may require a bit of digging, but if you research resources in your local area, you'll likely find additional tools for staying abreast of happenings in the media.

You can also keep your ear to the ground by maintaining close relationships with journalists and other PR professionals. Joining listservs of fellow public relations professionals also helps make certain you're receiving timely information on journalists' career transitions. You can find PR listservs by talking to other PR professionals. If you're a member of the Public Relations Society of America, the National Association of Black Journalists, the National Association of Hispanic Journalists, ColorComm, or other professional groups for journalists and public relations professionals, you can also join their listservs. You can also create your own online groups through Google Groups, Facebook, or Yahoo! Groups. If you are creating your own listserv, identify communications staff who work for organizations like yours and then invite them to join the group.

Last, with the advent of digital media it's easier to know where journalists are employed. By following reporters who cover your issues on Twitter and Facebook, and expanding your networks to include journalists on LinkedIn, you'll be better apprised of where a given reporter is working. (For more on social media, see Chapter 6.) Being in the loop on this sort of information helps you project an image as sharp, credible, and in the know. Such a reputation will help you to better promote organizational goals and objectives. It also helps you to be more effective.

Credibility in Action

In 2013, I was the lead communicator tasked with promoting litigation my organization, Advancement Project, filed against the state of Wisconsin. Advancement Project sued the state of Wisconsin under Section 2 of the Voting Rights Act for making it harder for African Americans and Latinos to vote. At the time, few organizations were bringing voting rights challenges under Section 2 of the Voting Rights Act, which required litigants to prove "impact" versus "intent" to discriminate. Most brought lawsuits under Section 5—before it was gutted in the U.S. Supreme Court decision *Shelby County v. Holder.*

I had pitched the *Washington Post* and the *New York Times* editorial boards to write about the case, and *New York Times* editorial board member Jesse Wegman called me back requesting more information about the distinction between Section 2 and Section 5. He particularly wanted to understand the "intent" versus "impact" distinction. Rather than attempting to explain the complex legal provisions of the voting rights measure, I enlisted the support of the lead attorney on the case, James Eichner. I arranged a media call with Eichner and Wegman so Eichner could answer the technical questions about the case. This ensured Wegman had accurate information in advance of writing an editorial on the matter. Bringing in a legal expert really helped to bolster my credibility. First, it was great that Wegman had enough respect for me to call and ask for more information. Second, I didn't attempt to make up an answer to a technical question that could have led to Wegman getting an incomplete picture of the legal issues at hand. And third, I made Wegman's job easier by providing him with a legal expert who he (and readers) could trust to use for information in his editorial.

Be Creative

Ever heard the expression "Ask and you shall receive"? While the phrase is taken from the Bible, it clearly applies to more than just spiritual matters. I firmly believe the reason so few people achieve great things is because they fail to imagine—or believe—that great things are possible. When you fail to conceive, you invariably fail to try.

For over two years, I'd worked with a group of youth who were members of Tenants and Workers United (TWU) and were seeking to implement Restorative Justice in their schools. Restorative Justice is a community-building and dispute-resolution tool that allows one to learn from and make amends for mistakes. The practice can repair a school community because it allows both the person who has created harm and the person who has been on its receiving end to reconcile.

Concerned about racial disparities in school discipline, the young people (with the assistance of TWU) embarked on a path to bring Restorative Justice to their schools. The school system expressed a commitment to the approach but offered what students saw more as platitudes than substantive change. We'd garnered some media attention in the *Washington Post* and in the local Alexandria paper, but we needed to make a bigger splash.[1] At the same time, I was short-staffed and out of budget. So, I decided to host what I called a pitch-a-thon. I trained the group of youngsters on how to pitch reporters and worked with them to practice actual pitches. It was a huge success. They even managed to engage a few reporters on the issue, including Khalil Abdullah, formerly of New America Media; and David Coles, a producer with PBS's *Newshour*. This approach stood out to reporters for its novelty: reporters don't often hear from youth who can concisely explain who they are, why they're calling, and why the journalist should care. It is a prime example of creativity on a budget, and I will try this approach again in the future.

Another opportunity for being creative involves the method you select to share information. Using social media tools to share information can be a creative approach. I discuss social media in greater detail in Chapter 6. In an attempt to highlight complex information or present information in visually appealing ways, many organizations repeatedly turn to infographics. For example, I wanted to document the various threats voters of color might face at the ballot box, so I hired Design Action Collective to develop a visually appealing infographic.[2] The infographic, which cost under a thousand dollars, could be quickly shared on various social media platforms, such as Twitter and Facebook. Infographics are also useful in TV segments since broadcast media places a premium on communicating through visual means. I've also used infographics to document the school-to-prison pipeline and the impact it has on students. In short, infographics are a visual way to explain complex information. They are an appetizer of sorts and provoke further study.

Being creative is not just something you should do. It's something you *must* do. Having noteworthy campaigns is of little consequence if the public doesn't know those campaigns exist. The *Guardian* reported in April 2014 that the ratio of public relations professionals to journalists is 4.6 to 1.[3] Creativity is the way to break through in the media. To get anywhere in this business, you must distinguish yourself and your organization. And while being creative could mean hiring a big-budget communications agency to design a campaign that really pops, you have other options. The keys to being creative have nothing to do with budget. It's about challenging yourself, thinking big, and being bold.

Challenge Yourself

The first step to being creative is challenging yourself to conceive. Set a goal of trying something new each month, whether it's reaching out to a new reporter or media outlet or creating a different kind of media piece outside your skillset. If you achieve the goal, find a small way to reward yourself. Then repeat the process until trying new things becomes second nature.

On a regular basis, I allow myself time to conceive, time to think of what's possible. I make a list of my goals for a given period—some attainable and some mildly unrealistic. The mildly unrealistic or difficult-to-achieve goals sometimes become possible with persistence and hard work. The stretch goals may appear implausible but some may be attainable. They all push me to keep trying. And here's the thing: if I'm successful, even a small victory will buoy my confidence. The boost encourages me to work even harder.

One area of challenge is stepping out of your comfort zone to engage reporters you may not know as well. As a manager, it's infuriating beyond belief to listen to communications professionals recommend the same reporters over and over without at least trying to reach others who may be interested in the story.

I can appreciate the alluring temptation of comfort and familiarity. I know it's often easier to pitch the same network or beat reporters who typically cover your issue. For instance, if you're in a racial justice organization, it can be tempting to think the only ones who care about racial justice issues are people of color or progressive media outlets. If this thought process sets in, you might start limiting your pitching solely to progressive and racial justice bloggers and reporters. Or, maybe you've had prior success with a particular outlet or reporter. It is true that it is often easier to go with the same batch of friendly reporters each time an issue in their subject area arises. While it's nice to start with the people you be-lieve will care about and cover your issue, I'm urging you to challenge yourself. As important as it is to touch this demo-graphic, there are additional people worth engaging as well.

Perhaps your employer or client wants you to successfully

pitch C-SPAN on livestreaming an important court hearing, rally, or event. Unless the event promises tens of thousands of people and is major in scope, most media outlets charge a fee to livestream an event. Your employer or client doesn't have funds to pay for the livestream and wants you to convince the outlet to do it for free. While you may not be able to convince a media outlet to cover the event for free if they are intent on being paid, the process of developing your best pitch and engaging them requires you to stretch. Occasionally, you may accomplish a stretch goal if you continue to try. Or, as in the case of livestreaming an event, perhaps you'll identify a lesser known entity to do the livestream for you. Of course, securing a major media network to do so enables you to reach a broader audience. If you have a good story—one that defies expectation or contains an element of controversy—and you're engaging the press far in advance, you're in an excellent position to pitch all media outlets who cover that subject area.

Think Big

To conceive great things, you must first expand your thinking. That's hard for some of us. How do you think big when everything and everyone around you reminds you of the seeming impossibility of your goals? There's a beautiful quote by Nelson Mandela that sums this up precisely: "It always seems impossible until it's done." The quote is especially applicable for communications professionals who should be constantly thinking about ways to share their message to grab and sustain the attention of the media and the public they serve.

Unless you are already predisposed to creativity, you may have difficulty maintaining big-picture thinking. There is a way to recondition yourself, however. Surround yourself with a diverse group of people from inside and outside your organization. The people don't all have to work in the communications field; they just need to be creative and strategic. Engage people who accomplish great things. Ask them for their tricks of the trade or for recommendations of books you can read to develop your thinking.

Several years ago, I read a book I would not soon forget: *Never Eat Alone, Expanded and Updated: And Other Secrets to Success, One Relationship at a Time* by Keith Ferrazzi.[4] This *New York Times* best seller outlines concrete steps you can take to accomplish goals; it inspires me to be creative, persistent, and diligent in building and using personal and professional networks. I also routinely start my mornings by listening to YouTube videos of motivational speakers such as Les Brown and the Hip Hop Preacher, Eric Thomas. Both help me to remember that anything is possible and to bravely dream big.

If you surround yourself with people who think big you will find ways to incorporate this frame into your thinking. You will eventually think and do great things yourself. Moreover, the more you practice thinking big, the easier it becomes.

Be Bold

There will always be voices (internal and external) telling you why you cannot accomplish big things. Don't allow self-doubt or the opinions of others to prevail. Learn to silence them.

Let's say you want to meet with editorial board members at a local paper but are unsure they want to meet with you. Be bold and ask anyway. The worst they can say is no. Maybe you want to pitch a guest column to the *New York Times*, but you step back after considering the small number of unsolicited opinion pieces from nonprofit organizations that they publish. Well, if you do not make the effort, you have no hope of seeing your issue on the opinion pages. Rather than abandoning the idea, think about a high-profile messenger who the paper may be interested in publishing. Carefully review the pieces they publish to see what you can glean from them in terms of writing style, bylines that gain traction, and other helpful tips. But maybe you aren't aiming to get a piece published at all. Perhaps you'd like to pitch your principal or leader for Oprah's *Super Soul Sunday* but you have no idea where or how to begin. This was me.

I had Oprah on my list for months before I finally decided to get serious about pitching to her team. I asked a staff member for the contact information, and that person asked an external ally who surprisingly had and was willing to share this information. I pitched Oprah's then communications director, Chelsea Hettrick, in late October and then again in mid-November 2014. I received a phone call from a producer at Harpo Studios on December 19, 2014, to discuss my pitch.

When Hettrick called, I was on a flight and missed the call. We played phone tag but never ultimately connected. While my guest has yet to appear on the show, I believe it's only a matter of time before this dream comes to fruition. I will continue to pitch until it does. The point here is we never really know what's truly possible until we try. And trying doesn't cost a penny.

Implementation => Ideas

If I am a proponent of thinking big, then I am an unwavering disciple of tenacity when it comes to implementation. Some people think big ideas are the hard part. They're not. If you give me an hour to think, I'll give you half a dozen ideas that could be implemented. But what good are the ideas if you are not disciplined enough to put them into practice? In his book, *How to Become CEO*, Jeffrey J. Fox quotes Ted Levitt of Harvard Business School: "Creativity without implementation is irresponsibility." Fox echoes this sentiment: "Ideas are nothing without execution. So few people in a corporation actually execute ideas that the person who does becomes visible, and is often sought to do more."[5]

Fox isn't the only one to hold this view on implementation. In the book, *Not for Bread Alone*, Moe Foner similarly remarked:

> Ideas are the easy part. You can put a group of smart people in a room and come up with all kinds of fantastic concepts. The hard part is making them happen. When I first went to the

endowments in 1978, I'm sure they said to themselves, "We've heard this kind of stuff before, but not from a union. We'll give 1199 a shot because we need a labor program. But chances are this guy Foner will never do half of what he says he'll do." We proved the doubters wrong. We made all of those ideas work.[6]

How many people have you met who spend their time ruminating on one brilliant idea after another? In tragic instances, some of us even sit on those great ideas only to watch someone else come along with the chutzpah to put them into action and enjoy unparalleled success. This doesn't have to be your fate.

When I draft strategic communications and marketing plans, I am not doing so because I can't think of better ways to spend my time. I am doing so because I believe the plan, if followed, will make a measurable difference for the candidate or cause for which I am working. Therefore, I take implementation as seriously as strategic planning. To dream and not act is failure by another name.

It bears mentioning that some of us are hardwired to be creative, some to be detail oriented, and some to implement. Sometimes you find a single person who possesses these gifts. Often, that's not the case. As a communications strategist, you should assess the skills within your shop. Start with yourself: Where are you strongest? What are your deficiencies? Think about your team members: what are their individual skills? You can learn more about your team by conducting routine surveys.

Surveying the staff can be done through Survey Monkey;

simply design questions to assess how people feel about their roles and whether they believe their skillsets are being maximized. Here's a possible survey:

- Tell me about a time you thrived in communications.

- What skillset do you pull on to thrive?

- Do you feel your skills are being fully utilized?

- What aspect of your job is most rewarding?

- What aspect is least rewarding?

- Do you have passions and interests that are not presently being tapped? If so, what are they?

- Do you feel you're in the right position? If yes, why? If no, what would you like to do if there were an opportunity?

Their responses will help you understand the resources you have internally and create an opportunity to have deeper dialogue with team members outside the context of deadlines or routine tasks. People are often multitalented, harboring a variety of interests and talents. I've often hired staff for one position and realized they had passions far greater than the roles for which they were hired. As I learn about my staff's interests and talents, I can determine what they bring to the team, and what I need to hire consultants for.

In 2015, I hired recent college graduate Drew Ambrogi to serve as a communications associate. In this role, Drew was responsible for building relationships with allies, writing press releases and other communications collateral, and pitching the media. When I interviewed Drew, I knew he had some experience with graphic design and video production, but I didn't realize this was his passion. After serving in the communications associate role for a year, Drew expressed a desire to transfer to a vacant digital media position. Once in the new role, he blossomed, creating engaging websites, graphics, memes, videos, and other digital tools. Upon discovering his skillsets, I realized I didn't need to have a graphic designer on a monthly retainer. I needed to hire design and video consultants only during crunch times when we had more work than one person could comfortably handle.

Once you've completed the assessment, your goal should be to fill in what's missing. If you don't have funds for a full-time staff person, consider bringing on an intern. Harvard College's Institute of Politics has a summer internship where the university pays the costs for the internship and looks for employers to provide fulfilling internship experiences. Other universities may offer something similar.

Creativity in Action

I gave myself the challenge of meeting with the *New York Times* editorial board because the paper plays such a pivotal role in shaping public perception. I carefully reviewed the editorial board section of the newspaper's website, scanning the respective board members to determine their areas of interest and who would be susceptible to a pitch on my issues: voting rights and overly harsh school disciplinary policies. I identified a couple of editors for each topic area then drafted a note pitching the idea. In this instance, my note was simply an invitation to sit down with me and discuss my organization's work. I tried to place myself in the editors' shoes and thought about whether I would be responsive to a pitch from a spin doctor, as public relations staff are sometimes called. I realized I needed to go BIG. I needed another important guest to make the meeting worth the editors' time, so I brought in the leader of the sprawling grassroots movement in North Carolina whom I mentioned earlier, the Rev. Dr. William J. Barber II. I refined my pitch note to illuminate the variegated and multi-issue campaign that Barber, an African American man of only forty-nine at the time, was leading in the South. I was firm in my belief that it was in the editors' best interest to meet not only with me and my organization but also with the leader of an organization that held massive weekly protests at a southern state capitol for more than a year. Of all the partners and groups I worked with, I believed Barber was unique in that the movement he was leading was multiracial, intergenerational, impactful, and bold. His Moral Movement was the perfect partner to highlight for this initial stage of relationship building because I knew the movement could benefit from exposure in a national paper such as the *Times*, and I believed the *Times* would want information on a movement that would have an impact on not just the South but states across the country. I wagered correctly. In the end, one of the members of the editorial board, Jesse Wegman, who covers voting rights, agreed to meet with me and my crew.

The conversation with Wegman was helpful. Since that February 2014 meeting, the editorial board has published several opinion pieces about voting rights in North Carolina, Wisconsin, and other states we discussed in the editorial board meeting. This tells me I targeted the right outlet for my cause as our interests regularly overlap. It also tells me there is a possibility of getting the New York Times to cover other voting rights issues.

Of course, my work hasn't stopped with that meeting, but that one on one was an important step. Although it took several editorials for the paper to begin mentioning my organization by name, our topics were being covered. This, in turn, allowed our fund-raising team to utilize the media clips and solicit funding to continue our work. It bears noting that when we weren't mentioned by name, I didn't become irate with my contact on the editorial board. I gently asked and encouraged him to include us by name in future editorial pieces.

Like many things in life, the sky is the limit; and if you aim for the sky, you may fall among the stars. The point is to try something new. Below are examples of creative and budget-friendly tips to garner media attention.

READ THE NEWS WITH THE INTENTION OF ACTING ON WHAT YOU'VE READ. Constantly ask yourself what you can do with the information you're receiving. Rather than reading an article and lamenting the current state of affairs, ask yourself what can be done. Should the article be shared with someone? Is the article missing an important component? Think about the action item, then do it. If you find, for example, the article is missing an important angle or voice, consider writing a letter to the editor (LTE) or a guest column highlighting the information you believe has been omitted.

USE A VIDEO TO SHARE YOUR MESSAGE. Rather than sending a press release to promote your issue or cause, consider developing a short one- or two-minute video. You could also create and then pitch (to media outlets) an opinion editorial or guest column.

PROMOTE WITH YOUTUBE. Consider recording short vignettes talking about your issue or cause and then promoting the videos via a YouTube channel or some other digital media platform. Videos are visual and compelling, and they allow people who might not take the time to read a one- or two-page press release (or a ten-page white paper) to learn about and become more engaged with your issue.

ORGANIZE A MEDIA CONFERENCE CALL OR WEBINAR. Rather than holding a press conference to announce a new report or campaign, consider organizing a media conference call or webinar. Media conference calls and webinars are convenient alternatives to press conferences. Attendees don't have to leave their offices to attend. They save travel time for already hurried reporters.

LAUNCH AN ONLINE PETITION. This is a good response to an infuriating action or to a comment that is homophobic or racist. Petitions may help you engage the media as well as appeal to a sympathetic public. They also expand an organization's email list.

USE TWO METHODS AT THE SAME TIME. Couple a media conference call with a Twitter Townhall or a Google Hangout. This will allow you to reach an even larger audience.

TARGET BOTH TRADITIONAL AND DIGITAL MEDIA. Layer all traditional media (press releases, press conferences, media conference calls, etc.) with digital media (online graphics, infographics, Google Hangouts, etc.). In other words, don't develop a communications plan that is narrowly focused on traditional media unless your target audience is a group that primarily receives their information from traditional means.

USE STORIFY. If you decide to organize a Twitter Townhall, consider creating a Storify to capture and articulate the essence of your message. The Storify can be shared with reporters and allies who were unable to participate but interested in the content from the online chat.

CREATE A WEBSITE TO SHARE INFORMATION. Race Forward, which utilizes research, media, and practice to advocate for racial justice, created Clocking In, a digital project to document "how people of color and women make up the majority of the low-wage workforce in restaurant, retail, and domestic industries and are disproportionately affected by unfair policies and practices related to wages, hours, mobility, and benefits."[7] By clicking on different portions of the animated video, website viewers learn about the low-wage workforce. You can explore the tool by going to https://clockingin.race forward.org/. But remember, a website can be as simple and inexpensive or complex and costly as you want it to be. You don't have to invest as many resources as Race Forward did to get your message across. And if you have someone with web design experience on your team, a website can be a very cost-effective way to promote your cause to anyone with an Internet connection.

UTILIZE OTHER VISUALS SUCH AS PICTURES AND VIDEO. With smart phones and related technology, it's easy to capture or record quality photos and videos. Here's an example: I was in North Carolina covering the NC NAACP's first Moral Monday rally on April 29, 2013. I pitched the event to state and national media prior to the demonstration, but the press advisory I sent prior to the event got very little traction. Undeterred, I went to the event armed with a cell phone and camera. I took pictures of the protestors, including Marty Belin, who uses a wheelchair. You can guess my surprise when Belin was arrested. I snapped a photo and sent it off with a short note to reporters. The subject line for the email was "North Carolina Police Arrest Woman in Wheelchair." The visual of a woman in a wheelchair being arrested was enough to capture the attention of news site *Think Progress*, which boasts millions of unique views per day. One *Think Progress* reporter, Ian Milhiser, responded, "Wait, this woman is in a wheelchair and she's being arrested?" It was a priceless photo begging further explanation, and therefore elicited interest.

The photo allowed me a platform to share with the media background for the work the NC NAACP was doing in North Carolina. From there, we received a handful of media calls requesting information about the demonstration and the

North Carolina General
Assembly police arrest
Marty Belin, who had been
inside the North Carolina
Statehouse on April 29,
2013, participating in the
Moral Monday protest.
Photo Credit: Jennifer R. Farmer

woman in the wheelchair. I repeated the same cycle each week of the protest, looking for unusual ways to capture the attention of a hurried media.

Your goal as a PR professional should be to think of creative methods of capturing a reporter's or producer's attention to elevate your issue, organization, or grassroots campaign. But capturing their attention is only the first step. One of the keys to securing sustained media interest is making it as easy as possible for members of the media to cover your organization or campaign, as you will see in the next chapter, Be Responsive. Responsiveness takes many forms, but for the purposes of this work, it's about being timely, being thorough, and generally doing everything you can to support reporters as they cover the issues you care passionately about.

FOUR

Be Responsive

Communicators spend hours emailing and phoning reporters trying to get them to cover their stories. If you're lucky
enough to have a reporter call you, you should respond as
quickly as possible! When a reporter phones or emails, she
should get a response within minutes—five to ten minutes
preferably. Even if your response is a mere acknowledgment
of the reporter's or producer's call or email, it's important to
follow up quickly. Why? When a journalist or TV booking
producer calls you, they are also likely calling other potential
sources. Sometimes the trick to getting your group included
in the story is by being the first to respond.

When I was working with the Denver-based parent and
youth group, Padres y Jovenes Unidos, to promote an intergovernmental agreement with Denver Public Schools and
the Denver Police Department, Pam Martinez, co–executive
director of Padres (along with Ricardo Martinez), requested a
meeting with me to discuss her idea of a successful PR campaign around the rollout of the agreement. Pam had high

expectations that she communicated so everyone was clear where she stood. During the conference call, Pam articulated a desire to blanket both state and national press with news of the agreement with the hope that other school districts and community groups were emboldened to achieve the same thing. In response to her request, I promised to

- place an opinion editorial on the agreement bylined by Pam or Ricardo Martinez in the local paper, the *Denver Post*

- place another opinion editorial from leaders in the movement to end the school-to-prison pipeline in a paper outside of Denver

- organize a media conference with Denver Public School students and officials for the local media and a national press call for members of the media who couldn't travel to Denver for the actual signing of the agreement

- pitch a front-page feature on the agreement in the *Washington Post* (Side note: *Washington Post* education reporter Donna St. George wrote the story, and it was published the Sunday before the agreement was announced. Including the stories of multiple students, community leaders, and school officials, the front-page story turned out to be the crème de la crème of our communications outreach for the agreement. I go into more detail about this in the next chapter, Be Relentless.)

In all, I promised so much that my former colleague, attorney Jason Sinocruz, became fearful I was overcommitting myself. I was nervous as well. However, I knew what it would take to please my partner, and I knew the agreement deserved significant media coverage. Knowing exactly what we agreed to, it was easier for me to focus and be responsive to those promises. Once we developed the communications plan, I shared it with the partner and indicated the deadline for each deliverable. For me, being responsive boiled down to acknowledging all communications, learning as much as possible, following up, and, most important—having and sharing a plan. Luckily, I delivered on everything promised, and the media coverage of the agreement was extensive.

Acknowledge All Communications

When responding, my first goal is to acknowledge the request. I want the reporter to know I received her voicemail, email, or tweet, and will get back with her as soon as possible. I know reporters are often on short deadlines, and I don't want them to look elsewhere or go with another source. A quick email, text message, or phone call acknowledging the request and providing a time frame by which I'll follow up is helpful. This is beneficial for both the reporter and the PR pro. For the PR pro, it's easy to become preoccupied with pressing demands and forget to acknowledge a media request. By stopping and acknowledging requests when they come in, you increase the likelihood that you'll follow up—especially if you set a calendar invite reminding yourself to do so. For the reporter, you give them the courtesy of acknowledging their email or phone call and a promise to circle back.

Learn as Much as Possible

By promptly responding to the initial request for comment with an acknowledgment and a promise to quickly follow up, I gain time to determine what I want my response to be. First, I learn as much as possible about the interview topic and the reporter (or host, in the case of a radio or TV interview). I want to know the origins of the story, background on the journalist or TV host, and the angle for the story. Armed with this information, I'm able to (a) determine if the interview would be beneficial for my organization and in line with the stories or messaging we're pushing, (b) determine who from my organization is best equipped to speak with the reporter (assuming I decided to accept the request), and (c) identify the proactive messages I want to advance during the interview. Sometimes this process takes a few minutes; other times it can take a bit longer.

The sooner you acknowledge a media inquiry, the sooner you can decide to accept or decline the request. Not all media inquiries are created equal and, contrary to popular opinion, not all press is good press. You may not be able determine which request is beneficial without following up with the reporter or producer. Nonetheless, responsiveness involves more than determining which interview requests to grant or decline. You're striving to gain a reputation as reliable.

When the media phones, you want them to judge you as trustworthy. In turn, they may reward you with future calls and additional opportunities to have your organization's perspective included in stories.

Follow Up

Responsiveness is also needed following an interview or discussion with the media. After I arrange one on ones with reporters, editors, columnists, or TV producers, they may request links to reports or other information. (I seldom do one on ones with radio hosts, as they typically don't do long-form media reports.) Within twenty-four to forty-eight hours after the meeting, I work to compile the requested information and share it with the person who requested it. This helps ensure the wonderful idea you pitched moves from concept to reality. Note, however, that while you want to be responsive, you shouldn't sacrifice accuracy. If you're unable to promptly provide the requested follow-up materials, call the reporter or media outlet to give them a realistic timeline for when the material will be ready. The important thing is to be both responsive and accurate.

For me, the follow-up after an interview is time consuming yet exciting. I truly love it. There's something about delivering on a promise that fuels a sense of accomplishment. After a meeting, event, or discussion with a reporter, I find an excuse or reason to follow up. The follow-up could be sending the material the reporter or editor requested during the meeting. It could also be sending a simple thank-you note showing my appreciation for their time. In rare instances, depending on the nature of the meeting, I've also been known to send flowers. For instance, after MSNBC president Phil Griffin hosted my organization for an editorial board meeting with the producers from dayside programming, I sent him a bouquet of flowers.

Have a Plan

It should come as no secret that public relations professionals serve multiple constituencies. In addition to working with the media, PR pros also work with leaders in their own organizations, as well as external constituents. So the principle of responsiveness applies to internal and external stakeholders, as well as the media. For instance, when I served as communications director for SEIU District 1199 (WV/KY/OH), I was accountable to union staff, union members, and the media, as well as allied organizations. In my work with Advancement Project, my constituents included organizational lawyers and staff, partner organizations such as the NC NAACP, Tenants and Workers United, Padres y Jovenes Unidos, members of the media, and allies in the movement for racial justice. If I focused on being responsive to my colleagues alone, I would harm my relationship with our partners, the lifeblood of the organization. If I narrowly focused on the media, I would alienate partners and staff.

So what's the key to being responsive when one is dealing with competing demands? When it comes to working with organizational leaders and external stakeholders, I find it is easier to be responsive when I am working from a comprehensive communications plan that outlines core objectives, tactics for achieving those goals, and an agreement on what success looks like. I want to know what will make the partner or leader I'm working with happy from a communications standpoint. While this is time consuming, it proves beneficial. The cost comes in time spent up front but pays off later when I can easily prioritize opportunities and respond accordingly. If I am unclear of the expectations of partners, I cannot possibly meet their needs. Or I can set out on a path to accomplish certain goals, only to realize in the end that the goals I've accomplished are not actually ones that are important to the allies on whose behalf I am working. Moreover, once I know the goals of each ally, I am better able to prioritize the tasks depending on the delivery date for each.

It is often impossible to achieve success without first understanding what success looks like. Without an end in mind, there's no way to know where you're going or when you've arrived. You'd be surprised how many times communicators are given the vague assignment of promoting a campaign or generating media coverage without a corresponding discussion clearly articulating how to define success. Being tasked with "generating coverage" is squishy. It isn't a measurable goal. There have been many times in my career when I generated media coverage and patted myself on the back for what I thought was a job well done only to have people in the campaign lament the fact there wasn't more coverage. Often campaign leaders did not articulate specific goals in terms of volume and type of media coverage. I included the stories that appeared in small media outlets as part of a successful media campaign only to discover that the leaders were thinking exclusively of large national papers. Or the organizational leaders had one paper in mind as a media target but hadn't clearly communicated that desire to the press team. If the goal is to generate media coverage, decide what type of coverage is desired, how much of it is sufficient (e.g., is there a certain quantity of articles or TV hits?), and whether you are targeting traditional media, digital media, or both. You should also determine the desired media outlets for coverage (print, TV, radio, the web). Are your teammates seeking coverage in a particular print newspaper? Further, if you've been tasked with generating media coverage, know that all media opportunities (e.g., interview requests) aren't created equal. Rather than simply seeing your organization's name in lights, you want to see the group in lights for the right reason. If a reporter calls you requesting comment on an issue that may not advance company goals, it's okay to decline. For instance, there are times when we receive interview requests when the reporter wants us to critique another group or leader. Unless we have an axe to grind, and we rarely do, accepting the bait to criticize others distracts us from our mission and simply isn't worth the trouble.

Being clear about what success looks like saves loads of time and avoids confusion and disappointment. Your primary objective is to come to an agreement on what constitutes success at the outset so you can responsively pursue it.

Responsiveness in Action

When I worked with the Rev. Dr. William J. Barber II, whom I mentioned earlier, the big-picture goal was to encourage the North Carolina legislature to abandon an avalanche of regressive and extreme policies. A secondary objective was to ensure regressive policies weren't passed in a cloak of darkness, devoid of attention and public awareness. From a communications standpoint, success meant highlighting in the court of public opinion the destructive policies being put forth by the North Carolina legislature and the fusion movement that had emerged to challenge them. We wanted to ensure the story was not confined to the borders of Raleigh, where the weekly protests were held, or to the Tar Heel State for that matter. Instead, we wanted to share the movement with media outlets across the country. We also wanted to inspire activists in other states to begin challenging injustices in their own communities.

In figuring out how to tell and retell this story so that the campaign was successful, I had to think about the selling points of the movement as well as the architect of the movement, the Rev. Dr. Barber. From a media relations standpoint, he was a communicator's dream: a gifted orator, inspiring theologian, historian, and scholar. If we arranged the media interviews and appearances, he could easily score home runs. But first, we had to come to agreement on how to frame the work. Barber explained our work together in this way: "I challenged Jennifer on framing, and she skillfully heard me and allowed me to be myself. She also adjusted accordingly while teaching me and the staff foundational communications techniques."

The takeaway here is that I couldn't promote the movement without also promoting its leader. To do this, I had to understand his preferences for messaging and framing. For example, Barber was very clear from the beginning that we not describe our work or opponents from a political frame. We made a conscious decision to abandon political labels such as Republican and Democrat. I also had to remember that he was a pastor, scholar, and theologian, and give him the freedom to communicate in a way that was true to his calling.

To be responsive to our campaign leaders and ensure regressive policies weren't passed without widespread attention, we needed to develop a multipronged campaign that included informing the public of the legislature's restrictive policies, as well as of the entities leading the pushback. We had to consistently garner national media coverage and ensure the movement was not characterized as a fringe or isolated protest. The fact that protests recurred weekly helped tremendously because it gave us multiple opportunities to attract media attention. The continual protests allowed more and more reporters from state, national, and international outlets time to cover the movement. Moreover, the weekly protests offered a sort of credibility. People covering the issue quickly came to realize the work in North Carolina wasn't a fly-by-night operation but a sustained campaign. Lastly, we were aided by the fact that the movement was racially, economically, and politically diverse.

A North Carolina State Highway Patrol trooper arrests a woman for participating in a protest organized by the North Carolina NAACP, as a General Assembly police officer monitors the crowd inside the rotunda of the North Carolina General Assembly building.

Photo credit: Jennifer R. Farmer.

To responsively meet the needs of my partner, I couldn't simply create a checklist and methodically cross off goals as they were achieved. I knew I had to spend time with Barber and his team to earn their complete confidence and trust. This couldn't be accomplished from my office in Washington, D.C. My team and I had to be on the ground in North Carolina. I needed to be immersed in the NC NAACP and have multiple conversations with Barber and his closest advisors. I made it my business to be there as much as possible and to have communications staff in North Carolina on occasions

Rev. Dr. Barber II with Mary Evelyn Rider O'Neil during one of the
Moral Monday protests at Bicentennial Mall in 2013, as Ms. Rosanell
Eaton (in black hat), a member of the NC NAACP, looks on.
Photographer and copyright owner: Phil Fonville, all rights reserved.

when I couldn't be physically present. For more than a year,
my former colleague Cynthia Gordy and I traveled to North
Carolina each week to be with Barber and his team and to
promote the weekly protests.

In the realm of communications, my task was to convince
state and national media that what was happening in North
Carolina was transformative, the beginnings of a moral
movement. To do this, I needed the work in North Carolina
to consistently make national news. I knew if the story was
limited to North Carolina, it would be hard to gain momentum and achieve the goals of the NC NAACP. It would be
easily dismissed by opponents. I wanted the eyes of the na-

tion to focus on North Carolina. Armed with a goal, I crafted a winning strategy to reach and engage state and national media.

While the work is far from complete, our communications support played a role in elevating the profile of Barber and the Forward Together movement. This has helped the group to hold elected leaders accountable. Moreover, after a lengthy three-year legal challenge to North Carolina's monster voter suppression law, the NC NAACP finally won the case in the Fourth Circuit Court of Appeals. The win can be attributed to many factors—skillful attorneys, wonderful witnesses and plaintiffs, a robust grassroots movement led by the NC NAACP—though our communications around and about the cases undoubtedly was a contributing factor.

Once a goal has been defined and you understand what success looks like, you can responsively map the plan to get there. You do not need a multimillion-dollar budget to be responsive. You'll need to check your email, cell phone, and social media accounts regularly to ensure you aren't missing media inquiries and communications from internal and external stakeholders.

In some cases, being credible, creative, and responsive isn't enough alone to tip the scales and garner media attention. When this happens, it usually indicates a need for persistence: sticking with your pitch, pitching different reporters at the same or different outlets, and generally never giving up. I'll elaborate more in the next chapter.

FIVE

Be Relentless

There's no escaping the fact that communications and public relations work involves an element of rejection. I can't tell you the number of times I've heard "no" from members of the media. For all the stories I've pitched and placed, there were countless others that were simply ignored. For all the meeting requests I've sent to media executives, editors, and reporters, many were flat-out denied, and in some cases, I didn't get a response at all.

Dealing with rejection is hard. But quickly overcoming rejection and being able to bounce back is critical in the communications field. Often communicators will experience "no" multiple times before finally getting a "yes." Bo Bennett's quote, "A rejection is nothing more than a necessary step in the pursuit of success," rings true. Moreover, after success, it's easy to be lulled into thinking every PR pursuit will be enthusiastically received.

One of my favorite journalists is Donna St. George, an education reporter with the *Washington Post* whom I mentioned

Student activists with Voices of Youth in Chicago Education attend a December 2012 U.S. Senate hearing on the school-to-prison pipeline organized by Sen. Dick Durban. Photo Credit: Jennifer R. Farmer

in the previous chapter. When I have an education-related story idea, St. George is often the first person I call. I met her in November 2012 while pitching a hearing Senator Dick Durbin of Illinois was organizing on the over-criminalization of youth of color in schools across the country. I got lucky on the first try and Donna covered the story and interviewed my former boss Judith Browne Dianis for the article. That article, " 'School-to-Prison' Pipeline Hearing Puts Spotlight on School Discipline," was published December 13, 2012.[1]

Encouraged by the victory, I waited a few weeks and pitched St. George on the historic intergovernmental agreement between Denver Public Schools and the Denver Police Department I've already discussed that limited the role of police in schools. Since St. George was the first reporter I called, I offered her an exclusive, meaning she would be the first reporter, and her outlet, the first outlet, to write about the story. This not only helped me, as the *Washington Post* is a respected national newspaper, but it also helped St. George to sell the concept of covering the agreement to her editor who needed to sign off. Media outlets want to be the first to break a story rather than jumping on a crowded bandwagon and covering stories other outlets have already covered.

In addition to offering St. George an exclusive, I also pitched her a full four or five weeks before the agreement would be signed. This allowed her time to think about whether she wanted to do the story, as well as time to convince her editor it was a story worth covering. Offering both notice and exclusivity solidified the deal. The *Washington Post* was the first media outlet to cover the historic intergovernmental agreement with St. George's February 2013 article, "A Shift in Denver: Limits on Police in Schools."[2] I was thrilled.

In addition to highlighting the critical agreement, I also positioned myself as a reliable and credible source. While I was off to a great start in building a mutually beneficial relationship with St. George, I quickly learned not all pitches would result in a story or an immediate one at that—sometimes it takes multiple pitches over many months to land a news article.

Motivated by two back-to-back successes, I thought all my future pitches to St. George would be a slam dunk. That wasn't the case; she declined several of my next pitches. However, I try not to take the word "no" personally. Instead, I listen to the feedback, try to grasp the lesson, and most of all, I bounce back. Of all the stories I've pitched to St. George, she's maybe covered only four. That's more than what I would have gotten had I not tried or stopped the first time I heard "no."

The person who internalizes rejection or is unable to overcome it may struggle with communications work. Communicators must be able to take rejection, distill the lesson in each experience, and then bounce back. And the reason they can consistently do so is because they believe in what they are pitching. If you're reading this book, it's because you want to be effective. It's because you want to use communications and public relations to create a more equitable world. Whether you are involved in environmental justice, securing LGBTQ rights, clearing barriers to the ballot box, ensuring racial justice, or seeking an end to the criminalization of youth of color, your end game is to make this world a better place. But there will always be forces against you that want to preserve the status quo. You will hear "no" from adversaries as well as allies who are preoccupied with other things. Being able to overcome rejection is key to accomplishing our goals.

When I consider communications professionals who consistently push through the word "no," one person fits the profile perfectly: Gebe Martinez-Johnson, whom I once supervised as a deputy communications director for the Service Employees International Union. She can be described only as relentless. Martinez-Johnson was a communications staffer for SEIU's immigrant justice campaign and currently runs her own PR consulting business. I'm not sure the word "no" registers in her psyche. She was relentless in her communications-related work for immigrant justice. Martinez-Johnson was among the first in the office and often the last to leave. She would pitch and place stories with reckless abandon. If she decided a story needed to be shared, she would move heaven and earth to ensure the world heard it. Sometimes this meant working to place a story six to eight weeks prior to when she wanted it to appear in print. Her enthusiasm couldn't be overlooked and her focus was not easily broken. She embodied the type of commitment many aspire to but few attain.

Distill the Lesson

Even with hearing a "no," sometimes there's a silver lining. In saying "no," a reporter might give you a glimpse into the types of stories they are interested in covering in the future, or they might direct you to a colleague who might be more likely to cover your issue. Sometimes a "no" today does not mean a "no" a couple months from now. The "why" behind the "no" is important.

For instance, I asked a former member of my team, Victoria Wenger, to pitch the *Washington Post* on a guest column about the systemic oppression of Native Americans, citing the Washington football team name as an example. The *Washington Post* declined to publish the piece. I asked Wenger to call the opinion page editor Michael Larabee and politely ask the reason for his decision. He graciously offered that the piece was beautifully written but submitted too close to the desired publication date. Our piece was submitted for consideration the Tuesday before the Sunday we hoped the column would run, which was the opening day of the 2014 professional football season. That valuable information from Larabee helped me better establish internal deadlines to successfully place opinion pieces. However, even knowing Larabee's preferred timeline for opinion pieces was not a key to the city in terms of opinion essay placements. Even after we submitted opinion essays with more notice, he still frequently declined to publish them. We persevered.

As I discussed in Chapter 3, in the spring of 2016 I was working with Alexandria Teens United, a division of Alexandria-based Tenants and Workers United (TWU). The young people had been working to win implementation of Restorative Justice in their schools for years and while school officials signaled a commitment to implement the program, the students felt the implementation was moving too slowly. After a series of strategy sessions with the teens, we decided to express their concerns in an opinion essay. I worked with Salem Mesfin and Elizabeth Tibebu to document their thoughts in an essay and then asked my colleague Jeralyn Cave to pitch it to the *Washington Post*. Cave initially pitched the essay to Larabee, the opinion page editor, and despite giving him more than two weeks' notice, he declined to publish the essay. Undeterred, I asked Cave to pursue a different editor at the paper: local opinion editor Jamie Kiley. Kiley accepted and agreed to publish the piece. Had we stopped at the first "no," the essay would not have appeared in print.

In these and other regards, it is clear relentlessness is about patience and persistence. Had we not pressed for an answer, we may not have known the *Post*'s desired lead time for non-urgent opinion pieces. Even when Larabee declined to publish the initial essay on the Washington football team, we knew it was a good essay and continued pitching it to other national media outlets. Had we stopped at the first, second, or third "no" (we pitched the piece to the *National Journal*, POLITICO, and the *Washington Post* before finally getting to "yes" with MSNBC), our piece, "This Football Season, Let's Wipe 'Redskins' from our Vocabulary," would never have been placed.[3]

The TWU students' opinion piece, "Students Seek Justice in Alexandria," presented another learning lesson in relentlessness. Sometimes the key to breaking through in the media is trying different reporters or editors at the same publication. The bottom line is failure is never an option. Failing to place an opinion piece is losing a golden opportunity to share your message. Opinion pieces allow commentary (i.e., your message) to be shared directly with readers and, as an earned media tool, can be published without a corresponding price tag. The only cost is the time it takes to write the essay and ensure it is published. In this way, stopping at "no" is unacceptable.

Relentlessness is about seeing denial as a temporary rather than permanent fixture. It's about viewing a "no" as an opportunity to tweak and refine. It's also about refusing to take denial as rejection, which is personal. My work is professional; therefore, I cannot experience rejection for my work, only denial. This shift in perspective enables me to better cope with the obstacles that invariably come. Furthermore, just because a reporter or producer doesn't bite on a story idea today, doesn't mean the idea is permanently doomed.

When you hear the word "no," try to determine the reasoning behind it. Is the topic you're pitching not the reporter in question's area of interest? Is the reporter or editor bogged down—as they almost always are—with other projects? Is the reporter or editor traveling or have they been assigned to another story? If the answer to any of these questions is yes, it may be possible for your story to be covered later.

For instance, on July 21, 2014, I took my former boss at Advancement Project, Penda D. Hair, to meet with Richard Wolf, a *USA Today* reporter who covers the Supreme Court. We discussed an upcoming preliminary injunction hearing for the lawsuit Advancement Project filed on behalf of the North Carolina State Conference of the NAACP against North Carolina's voter suppression measure as well as our lawsuit against Wisconsin's voter ID law. My desired outcome was an article timed with the impending decision, following a preliminary injunction hearing that was held July 7, 2014. Wolf shared that he was heading out for a two-to-three-week vacation and could not commit to doing the story in my desired time frame but he did express interest in writing an article on voting rights legal challenges that might ultimately reach the U.S. Supreme Court. I thanked him for being so gracious with his time, shared as much information as possible, then scheduled a reminder to touch base with him once he returned from vacation.

After this initial meeting, I downloaded the highlights

with my team, offering insights on the ideal piece Wolf would be interested in writing. A short time later, we discovered the federal voter ID case we won against Wisconsin's restrictive voter ID law was being appealed and could likely end up at the Supreme Court. We made a note to pitch Wolf a couple weeks prior to the September 12, 2014, oral arguments during the appeal hearing. This was an opportunity to strike while the iron was hot since our case could be going to the Supreme Court. We pitched Wolf again, this time offering plaintiffs and witnesses who could speak to the difficulties many voters would face should the victory be overturned on appeal. Seeing a path to the Supreme Court, Wolf wrote the story, "Voting Rights Cases May Be Heading Back to Supreme Court," two months after my initial pitch.[4]

This was a long, multi-month process, but my team and I didn't take no for an answer nor did we allow Wolf's vacation to be a deterrent. We simply worked around the vacation and used the initial "no" to think through a better approach. This is a clear-cut example of what it means to be relentless. It's also an example of extraordinary PR on an ordinary budget since we re-pitched the story idea once the appeal made it more newsworthy. It bears noting that these examples have less to do with up-front costs, such as advertising, and more to do with timing as an important factor for propelling news stories.

Knowing When to Back Off

There is a fine line between not taking no for an answer and becoming downright annoying. When a producer or reporter gives me an outright no, I will accept it but try to glean enough information to help me tweak or alter my pitch for other reporters or for future use. If the reporter or producer gives me an outright "do not call me again"—which seldom happens—I will back off in terms of pitching the issue or event for which they were uninterested. Alternatively, I may pitch someone else at the outlet. Notice, I didn't say I would back off entirely in terms of abandoning the issue or reporter in question. Another issue could come up that could be more to their liking and I may reach out to them at another time. While it's important to be tenacious, the goal is not to gain a reputation of being a stalker. I'll undoubtedly need to pitch the same reporter again on a different topic in the future, and I want them to take my phone call and respond to my emails.

Keep Believing

The key to being relentless is believing in something bigger than ourselves. When we believe in something bigger than ourselves, we're likely to stick with it. We're passionate when we talk about it, and that passion is contagious. When you truly believe in something, you will go to the ends of the earth fighting for it.

A memorable time when I experienced being connected to work that was much bigger than me was in North Carolina in 2013. I'd run the Nike women's half-marathon: that's 13.1 miles. After my run, I wanted to do nothing more than go home, shower, sit on the couch, and devour a *huge* cupcake, the biggest one I could find. The problem is I pledged to attend a planning meeting with the Rev. Dr. William J. Barber II of the North Carolina State Conference of the NAACP to learn more about a protest at the state capitol the following day. Having just run my heart out, I wasn't the least bit excited about flying to North Carolina that afternoon. Nevertheless, I gave my word that I would be there, promising to both learn about the work in North Carolina and offer communications support. I was tired when I arrived, but by the time I left the Davie Street Presbyterian Church in Raleigh where the pre-demonstration service was being held, I was completely energized.

At Davie Street, I witnessed the greatest display of compassion and camaraderie among people who were young, old, black, white, gay, straight, Christian, Muslim and many others, some of different faiths and some who professed no faith at all. I had never seen such brotherly love in my entire life. These people treated each other with remarkable love and respect. They were a family united in a belief that their state needed a change. They wanted to protect voting rights, health care, quality education, and good jobs, and they were determined to go to the Statehouse every Monday for what later became known as Moral Monday protests. From my first encounter in that church, I was sold hook, line, and sinker. From that point on, I decided I would do whatever was necessary to support the movement. I flew back and forth from Washington, D.C., to North Carolina to help promote and publicize the protests. I wanted people in Georgia, New York, Florida, and across the country to hear about this budding movement. On occasions where I couldn't physically be in

North Carolina, I sent my deputy Cynthia Gordy, who was based in New York City. I worked the phones, calling producers, reporters, bloggers, and anyone who would listen about the movement to hold elected leaders accountable. I took and shared photos and video footage to give those who were not in North Carolina a sense of what was happening. It all seemed surreal and exhilarating.

The protestors—many of them doctors, nurses, teachers, students, and other respectful citizens—who entered the Statehouse to pray, sing, and meet with their legislators, were charged with trespassing and disturbing the peace. Imagine going into your legislator's or employer's office to raise an issue and being not only disregarded but *arrested*. That's the position in which these peaceful protestors found themselves. However, they vowed not to give up. They came back week after week, and with each subsequent week, they came back with friends, family, and allies. The crowds swelled. There were thirty people at the first protest on April 29, 2013. That figure multiplied to the tens of thousands in the space of just a few months. Each time they came back, my team and I came as well. We continued to help tell their story throughout the entire process.

I was relentless in advocating for them because I thoroughly believed—and still do—in the Rev. Dr. Barber, his team, and the courageous people participating in the Moral Monday protests. Relentlessness in telling the story of the Moral Monday protests wasn't just about repeatedly pitching it. It was also about using every mode of traditional and digital communication to promote the work. All of our press releases were accompanied by videos, photos, and visual demonstrations of what it was like to be in North Carolina advocating for and with the people of the state. We knew visuals could tell the story far better than text, and Barber rightly relied on videographers and photographers to help communicate the essence of our movement. At the very first protest, I remember watching a woman being arrested in a wheelchair. The only way to communicate the injustice of this was to take a photo, as I mentioned in Chapter 3 on being creative. While there were just thirty of us there, I snapped a picture of a state trooper arresting Marty Belin and sent it to Ian Milhiser at *Think Progress*. He quickly responded and wrote a story about the basis of the protests and the unfolding events.

What I learned from this experience is that you cannot effectively promote something that you do not actually embrace. If you believe in something, you'll stick with it even when the going gets tough. You'll think of creative angles to share your work. You'll fly from D.C. to North Carolina or from New York City to North Carolina on a weekly basis for it. It is easy to lay your all on the line once you have a firm belief in the issue in which you're involved.

Relentlessness in Action

When I worked for Advancement Project, we hired the California-based media production company Wondros to produce a video detailing the devastating impact of the school-to-prison pipeline. In the video, we featured Kiera Wilmot, the seventeen-year-old honor student who was handcuffed,

Kiera Wilmot, left,
and her twin sister,
Kayla Wilmot.
Photo credit: Marie Wilmot.

arrested, and expelled over a science project gone wrong, first mentioned in Chapter 2. I raise the video again now because it pertains to relentlessness. While the short segment was compelling and interesting, I initially struggled to find a news hook to make it of interest to reporters and producers outside of Florida until Kiera graduated from high school. Many reporters and media outlets enjoy feel-good stories with a happy ending. With that in mind, I reasoned the most opportune time to release the video and discuss the school-to-prison pipeline was around the time of Kiera's graduation. Armed with a strong hook—an honor student who had been arrested and booked on felony charges for a science project gone wrong was graduating and heading to college—my traditional and digital media team went to work pitching the video.

I quickly drafted a pitch note for TV producers and a press

release for the broader media. Then to promote Kiera's story on various digital media platforms, I enlisted Danielle Belton, our digital media staffer (now the managing editor for the *Root*). We posted the video detailing her horrific experience on our YouTube page, sent a corresponding press release with a link to the video embedded in it, and then worked the phones, relentlessly calling reporters and producers and pitching them on the undeniable human interest story. In the space of just a few hours, the story was picked up by print and TV reporters alike. The YouTube video garnered more than 17,000 views in just a few days. Had we pitched and released the video to the media in April 2014 when it was completed, I'm confident we would have garnered very little media coverage. In this regard, relentlessness was about holding the video until current events—in this case, high school graduation—made it timely and then diligently pitching it.

Releasing the video around the time of Kiera's graduation from high school was a perfect example of extraordinary PR on an ordinary budget. The graduation presented an opportunity to share Kiera's story and highlight the problems with overly harsh school discipline and the school-to-prison pipeline. It is also an example of holding on to a good story until current events make it timely. Don't be afraid to refine your pitch or wait until a current news event makes it timelier and more likely to be picked up.

There are three big takeaways from this section. First, the key to breaking through in the media and elevating stories worth telling is to be relentless. Next, it's easier to be relentless when you believe in something bigger than yourself.

Believing in something bigger than yourself is being thoroughly convinced of the efficacy and value of what you're doing. When you do, nothing can separate you from your goals. Finally, be persistent, but not to the point of alienating members of the media.

As you incorporate the principles of being creative, credible, responsive, and relentless, remember you have power regardless of the size of your organization's PR budget. The advent of social media has really made it possible for all people and all organizations who wish to use it to share their message with a broader audience. It's a way of leveling the playing field.

SIX

Social Media
on an Ordinary Budget

There are some people who see themselves as social media enthusiasts. Others identify as traditional media specialists. I fall into the latter category. However, even traditional media specialists should have an understanding and appreciation for social media. Here's why.

Social media has been a significant boost to entities in the public and private sectors, not to mention to persons working in the communications and public relations industry. By social media, I am referring to sharing platforms such as Twitter, Facebook, Instagram, Snapchat, YouTube, Periscope, and LinkedIn, among many others. Many of us use these platforms to communicate who we are, what we care about, and what we believe others should know. Even celebrities and elected officials have found ways to use social media to bolster their personal brands and connect with followers and constituents.

Online social sharing tools are low-cost means of expressing thought leadership, discussing current events, and holding leaders, brands, and celebrities accountable. These tools are effective means of connecting with audiences who respond favorably to interactive visuals such as infographics, photo memes, and animated GIFs. Social media is increasingly important for communicators and public relations professionals, as social networking tools allow PR professionals and others to research journalists, editors, and producers, while quietly learning their likes and dislikes on a host of topics. By following reporters on Twitter, Instagram, or Facebook, public relations professionals can get a sense of the issues they cover and ones that are of personal interest.

Choose the social media platform that best fits your goal. They all have strengths and limitations that lend themselves to different kinds of communications.

- Facebook allows for more personal interactions as users, reporters included, tend to make more intimate disclosures about their families, personal lives, travel schedules, and other information that one might glean otherwise only through personal relationships with the journalist or producer. With more than 1.59 billion monthly users as of December 2015, *Adweek* declared Facebook the king of social media platforms.[1] As of February 2017, that number has grown beyond 1.8 billion.[2]

- Periscope and Facebook Live, two leading mobile live-streaming services, allow users to broadcast events or speeches to a broader audience beyond those who physically attended the event or speech. This gives event organizers a broader reach in terms of sharing their message.

- LinkedIn, which boasts 433 million monthly users, not only allows users to connect with persons in their professional networks, but it also has a publishing feature, PULSE, which allows users to publish blog posts and essays that can then be shared with their networks.

- Twitter enables users to share news stories while making quick, punchy comments on any number of topics. Twitter is also useful in terms of tracking reporters' employers and beats. For example, you can type in a reporter's or producer's name and learn who they work for and, sometimes, their assigned beat. Why is this important? Every communicator has had the experience of attempting to contact a reporter at his or her media outlet only to receive a bounceback email informing them that the reporter is no longer employed there. By doing a quick search on Twitter (or LinkedIn for that matter), you may determine the reporter's current employer. Twitter boasted 320 million monthly users as of March 2016, according to *Adweek.*[3]

- If the target audience for your organization is high school or college students, Instagram and Snapchat may be more appealing, since young people use the platforms in record numbers. *Adweek* noted Instagram had 400 million monthly users as of September 2015.

While blogging is not a social media platform, it can be an effective way to create and distribute thought leadership online. Blogging is a way of promoting one's message and can be shared on an organization's blog, through blogging sites—such as Huffington Post and Medium, or through other social media sites, like Facebook and LinkedIn.

In sum, social media allows users to communicate with people who would otherwise be off limits. Prior to social networks, public relations could easily interact only with journalists whom they knew or journalists whose contact information was readily accessible. Thanks to social media, PR pros can interact with anyone who has a public presence on social networks.

One of the most appealing aspects of social media is that it is low cost. Other than staff time, it costs nothing to develop and schedule Twitter or Facebook posts about your issues. Using Periscope and Facebook Live requires a reliable Internet connection or data usage on your cellphone plan (and plenty of battery life or a charger for longer broadcasts). The costs associated with increased data usage can usually be submitted for reimbursement to your clients or employer, though this should be discussed and approved in advance. Assuming you have or can raise a modest budget of a couple hundred dollars, communicators and small businesses can also take advantage of low-cost Facebook or Twitter advertising to promote reports, events, or campaigns.

Since social media tends to be more visual, infographics, photo images, memes, videos, and GIFs tend to do well. Thanks to improvements in cell phone technology, most cell phones capture not just photos but also videos. This means anyone on your staff with access to a functioning smart phone can assist your organization in sharing visually appealing content on social media networks.

For entities with limited coffers, social media presents an opportunity to elevate their messages to audiences that could previously be reached only with extensive advertising dollars. Online petitions, for example, can be created with little resources—nothing more than the staff time that it takes to create, post, and share the petition.

While I've outlined the numerous benefits of social media, I should also provide some context. Social media is rapidly evolving. Many of the platforms that exist today could be obsolete in a year. One of the keys to being effective on social media is keeping your ears to the ground in terms of identifying and learning about emerging trends. This will allow you to remain on the cusp of innovation while ensuring you can share the work of your organization through timely channels. Doing this requires being in touch with other communicators and social media experts, as well as reading PR blogs and other resources. Regardless of the platform, however, the four principles of extraordinary PR—be credible, creative, responsive, and relentless—always apply. Let's focus on the CCRR framework as a strategy to promote effective use of social media.

Credibility on Social Media

Social media is not without its caution. It has been said that it takes five minutes to ruin an organization's brand via traditional media: newspapers, TV, and radio. With social media, one can be compromised in the amount of time it takes to schedule a tweet or post a Facebook message.

How many times have we observed people making inartful, if not offensive, comments, only to quickly delete them after they cause backlash? In 2014, John Charlton, the associate director of media relations for the Ohio Department of Education, sent an inappropriate tweet in response to criticisms about charter schools in the state. The tweet promptly turned into a news story. Charlton wrote, "Guys, it's after 5 on Friday. Take a break from muckraking and enjoy the weekend. Maybe you can get laid. Lol."[4]

The goal of the PR staffer is to *make* not *become* the news. Rather than successfully handling the critique on charter schools, the media relations director took a personal jab at the critics. The personal jab led to future stories, not on the issue, but on the spokesperson's comments. This temporarily detracted from his administration's broader goal. This is a great example of why PR professionals should be careful to maintain their credibility on social networking sites.

Credibility means understanding that while we may maintain personal social media accounts, anything we say can generate critique for the organizations and companies that employ us. Inserting a tweets-are-my-own disclaimer does not give you carte blanche to say anything that comes to mind, nor does it fully protect the organization that employs you from careless comments you may make on your personal account or your employer's social media account. Moreover, if you commit a crime or are embroiled in a scandal, the media will want to know as much about you as possible. This includes your employer. In describing the incident, the media will invariably connect you to your organization because doing so offers context on who you are and what you're about.

In the aftermath of a video depicting former Baltimore Ravens player Ray Rice knocking his then girlfriend Janay Palmer unconscious, the hashtag #WhyIStayed took root on Twitter. The hashtag detailed why victims of domestic violence often stay with abusive partners. Survivors of domestic violence shared heartfelt and deeply personal stories for why they stayed with their abusers. Attempting to "newsjack" or capitalize on current events to elevate their brand, a tweet from the account of pizza-maker DiGiorno used the #WhyIStayed and added, "You had pizza."[5]

Domestic violence is deadly, and it is never appropriate to make a mockery of it. In this case, the person running the account probably attempted to cash in on a trending hashtag without thoroughly reviewing what the hashtag was about. It was a dark period for DiGiorno and a prime example of damaging one's credibility on social media.

Creative Uses of Social Media

Social media is time- and cost-effective, but you still need to be creative to stand out from the crowd. Being creative on social media can mean coming up with catchy hashtags and clever ways to say things, or using amusing or thoughtful GIFs that convey how you feel and what you want to say with a simple image layered with words.

In September 2016 Keith Lamont Scott was shot and killed by a police officer, prompting protests in Charlotte, North Carolina. I was working to highlight the experience of clergy who witnessed the fatal shooting of one of those protesters. The media was reporting that the shooter was a fellow protester, but some clergy members questioned that account. It was 9 p.m., far beyond the usual time for sending press releases. Nonetheless, I drafted a press release and distributed it through the normal channels to reach the media. The press release questioned police accounts of the shooters and identified clergy who were near the protest site in Charlotte and who were available for media interviews. One of our leaders, Pastor Michael McBride, took a photocopy of the press release and shared it on his Twitter account. Almost immediately, my phone rang with reporters and producers wanting to speak with the clergy leaders I'd referenced in my press release. From 10 p.m. to 1 a.m. I fielded interview requests and staffed actual media interviews. This technique of tweeting out the press release (in addition to sending it through the more traditional channel of email) proved incredibly effective. Notably, the cost was minimal, requiring just a computer, Internet connection, Twitter account, and time.

Relentlessness on Social Media

Relentlessness on social media is about tracking the journalists who write or report frequently on your issues. It's about ensuring your organization is utilizing the various platforms to elevate your issues and campaigns. It's about targeting influencers as well as journalists. By *influencers*, I am referring to people with large online followings who can influence others. Influencers can help you amplify a message by retweeting your tweets or liking and sharing your posts on Facebook.

On June 27, 2015, just a few days after a white man sat through a bible study at the Emanuel African Methodist Episcopal Church in Charleston, South Carolina, and then murdered nine African American churchgoers, Charlotte activist Bree Newsome traveled to South Carolina and removed the Confederate flag from outside the state capitol. Following her act of resistance, I drafted a blog post on women's leadership.[6] My essay was posted on Huffington Post, and I later tweeted it from my Twitter account. *Grey's Anatomy* actor and Advancement Project board member Jesse Williams then tweeted my blog post to his then 1.8 million followers. I received more retweets from his single tweet than I've ever had since opening a Twitter account in 2012.

Relentlessness is also about continually tweeting out and posting articles, editorials, and opinion essays that are favorable to your work. For example, once you land a story on a campaign, tweet the story out while tagging the reporter who wrote the story and the outlet that employs them. When you tweet or post the story don't focus just on the headline. Read the article and then tweet or post the most compelling piece of the story, something that would inspire readers to read the article or watch the media clip in its entirety. Further, if you or one of your principals has a TV interview, capture the interview and post it on your YouTube channel and Facebook page. This creates evergreen content and allows you to connect with a broader audience.

Responsiveness on Social Media

PR pros spend significant time chasing reporters and producers and trying to get them to focus on the issues they are promoting. By tweeting about our issues we can easily attract the attention of the media. Once their interest is piqued, reporters may request an offline discussion to receive information. I should note that I've received media inquiries after I've posted things on social media and also after my bosses or colleagues posted noteworthy items on social media sites, such as Twitter and Facebook.

Once a reporter or producer reaches out on social media, they should receive a timely response. If the topic they'd like to discuss is not one that advances your issue or cause, you might acknowledge their request and refer them to another organization for comment. Or, you might simply let them know that you have no one available to speak with them at that time. You could also try to get the reporter to pivot to an angle that is more closely aligned with your campaign or issue. You can do this by letting the reporter know that your spokesperson is not able to speak to the issue they've raised, but you'd be happy to discuss current campaigns. If the reporter or producer contacts you about something you've tweeted or said on a social media network, the interview should be a slam dunk—so long as your tweets are in line with your organization's position. (See the previous section on credibility.)

The Bottom Line on Social Media

At the beginning of this chapter, I mentioned that some of us see ourselves as traditional media specialists, and others, social media strategists. If you, like me, fall into the traditional media category, you should still incorporate social media into your communications outreach plans. I typically draft a communications plan, outlining campaign goals and the communications tactics I recommend to accomplish those goals. I'll then turn the communications plan over to the social media staffer for their input and feedback. This ensures a well-rounded communications approach.

The advent of social media has been a tremendous boon to PR professionals. I offer many examples of just how important it has been to the success of some of my campaigns not only in this chapter but throughout the book. By applying the CCRR framework, you can use social media platforms to elevate your message. You don't need a multimillion-dollar PR budget to find success in social media—or traditional media, for that matter. By utilizing social media platforms such as Facebook, Facebook Live, LinkedIn, Snapchat, and Twitter, you can invariably learn more about the reporters you are seeking to engage and further highlight your organization's work. The bottom line? Social media helps ensure you get your message out.

PR Tactics
on an Ordinary Budget

Tactics are the lifeblood of communications and public relations. They are the deciding factor in not only garnering media attention but also fulfilling campaign goals and objectives. By creating opportunities to highlight a campaign's objective, tactics ensure that neither the campaign nor its intended target is overlooked by the media. If my campaign goal is to ensure school disciplinary policies are uniformly applied in a school district, I may pursue a host of tactics, such as publishing a report detailing racial inequities in school discipline, publishing an opinion essay from a student or parent on their experience, staging a press conference involving all students, or meeting with the editorial board to share facts and findings pertaining to school discipline. In this regard, tactics are a means to the end, not the end itself.

In the preceding chapters, I focused on the principles for successfully promoting your issue, organization, or grassroots campaign: being credible, creative, responsive, and relentless. While tactics are decided by the respective campaigns and organizational culture, I want to share a small range of possible tactics you and your team might employ to garner positive media attention that will help reinforce for donors and constituents the efficacy of your organization and mission. This ensures you can continue to fulfill your mission over the long term.

As I walk through a variety of tactics, I'll also detail the principles that are most important for each tactic to underscore the CCRR framework.

TACTIC 1
Proactively Pitch Stories

A gardener plants seeds with the full expectation of a harvest. You cannot enjoy a harvest absent time tilling the ground and preparing the soil for the seed. Only once the ground is prepared and the seed is planted can you anticipate a harvest. From a communications standpoint, proactively pitching a story is a lot like planting seeds. It involves thinking through potential story ideas, news hooks, and the time frame you want your story to run. While the publication date is ultimately determined by the editor and publisher, you should have a general sense of when events in the future might make a story on your topic more relevant. On the contrary, sometimes you may want to share information with reporters without expecting a story in return—at least not right away. Periodically reach out to reporters, editors, and producers to share information on issues they cover or are passionate about in order to keep you and your issues top of mind. I occasionally send articles, reports, or links to TV segments on issues when I know a reporter, editor, or producer may have interest.

While communications entails an element of passivity—since communicators must react and respond to media inquiries—you should proactively pitch reporters, editors, and radio and TV producers. If you wait for reporters to contact you, you'll be waiting a long time and get few stories placed in the process. Or the stories you are contacted about will do little to advance the narrative or message you are working to promote.

When reporters contact sources, they are usually working on a particular story with a particular angle. When I worked for Advancement Project, I routinely received four to five media requests per week. Many fell right in line with my work, but some did not. While I work to be as accommodating as possible, if I am not proactively pushing my own organization's agenda, our narrative will not be elevated. While it's sometimes good to occasionally accept unsolicited media requests, doing so may not advance your issue. In other words, you'll be playing on someone else's court.

To proactively pitch a story idea, you need an understanding of which reporters cover which topics. Prior to pitching, research your media target and get a sense of the types of issues they cover, as well as the stories they've recently covered. If your organization focuses on mass incarceration, research media articles and determine which reporters are writing about the topic or related topics. Equipped with this information, you can target the appropriate media contacts and craft a more effective pitch. A pitch can be delivered via email, on the phone, or by voicemail.

There are several types of pitches. One is sent for long-term stories when you are sharing information in the hopes of getting a story at some point in the future. Alternatively, a pitch can also be delivered in anticipation of an upcoming event, such as the release of a report or a major announcement. A pitch that is shared for a future report or story idea is proactive in that you are planning weeks, sometimes months, in advance.

Proactively pitching stories takes on other forms as well. Advancement Project's core issues include voting rights, voting rights restoration for persons with prior felony convictions, eliminating the over-criminalization of youth of color in schools across the country, and ending racial disparities in school discipline. On any given day, my team and I were facilitating media events on one or more of these topics. While my natural pitch list for an announcement pertaining to school discipline included education reporters from various outlets, I occasionally planted seeds of information with education editors as well as editorial board writers who focused on education from various newspapers. I didn't expect the editors or editorial boards members to cover every story idea. However, I wanted them to think of me and call me prior to writing or editorializing on an education story, or any of the other issues my organization covered, for that matter. This was a no-risk, no-pressure pitch. I had already developed my targeted pitch list, and anything extra was a bonus.

The pitching strategies I mentioned earlier worked well

for me. Of course, there are other options. I learned one while working as a legislative agent (lobbyist) for the Ohio Department of Transportation under former Ohio governor, Ted Strickland. The Strickland administration was pushing a high-speed rail project connecting some of Ohio's largest cities: Cleveland, Columbus, Cincinnati, and Dayton. While it was an exciting time, we were constantly beset by negative press and hostility from policy makers. We were often forced to explain the value of the train project. I quickly realized that one communications professional–turned lobbyist was spending hours on end phoning reporters to disparage our efforts. This resulted in dubious stories and distortions about our project. While this was a distraction for the administration, I marveled at the approach, vowing to appropriate a similar tactic of pitching reporters and peppering them with different ideas for future articles.

HOW TO DO IT

BE CREATIVE. When I draft the original pitch and subsequent pitches, I try to identify as compelling and interesting a subject line as possible. I'm looking for a subject line that begs a reaction. Here's the catch though: I'm not interested in bait-and-switch tactics in which I use a provocative headline that leaves reporters, editors, and producers let down after they open the email. Instead, I'm looking for something that will entice them to read my message.

BE RELENTLESS. When I pitch, I typically send the pitch via email first and then follow up with a phone call. In most cases and when time permits, I'll give the reporter a couple days to review my email or listen to my message. Then if I haven't received a response, I'll follow up again with another email or voicemail message.

Speaking of email, there is some disagreement over whether email is preferred to phone pitches. In many cases, I'll do both. I will craft a carefully worded, informative pitch and send it via email. However, sending an email can be passive, and I don't want to rely on the reporter to see my email and then respond. Sometimes I will also leave a voicemail message calling attention to the emailed pitch. When I leave a message, I am essentially repeating my pitch. Sometimes this works. I once pitched Ed Schultz—who at the time had a show on MSNBC—on a senate hearing organized by Illinois senator Dick Durban about school discipline and the school-to-prison pipeline. I left an impassioned message on Schultz's cell phone, and much to my surprise, he called back within thirty minutes and covered the hearing the very next day.

Regardless of the preferred format for sending pitches, the follow-up is incredibly important. Reporters' inboxes are inundated with press releases, white papers, and other material. More than half of the information is not relevant to the topic the reporter covers on a day-to-day basis. The blog *Ragan's PR Daily* estimated the three largest press release distribution services sent more than 642,000 press releases in 2013.[1] This doesn't include the smaller distribution services; nor does it include organizations that don't use press release distribution services. If you factor in the decline of staff in many newsrooms and the fact that there are far more public relations professionals than there are journalists (remember, PR reps outnumber journalists 4.6 to 1), you'll begin to gain an appreciation for the importance of crafting a winning pitch and the art of the follow-up.

Given these dynamics, I'm sure you can appreciate how easy it is for some messages to get overlooked. Additionally, if a reporter is bogged down covering another assignment, they may lose sight of or not have an opportunity to review or respond to your inquiry. Remember, a lack of an immediate response doesn't always signal a lack of interest. That's why gentle email or voicemail reminders are helpful. In some cases, the journalist may see the pitch but want to refer it to someone else in the newsroom who either is more inclined to do a story or may be able to get to the story sooner. They could also refer it to a colleague who has a history of covering the topic or ones like it.

BE CREDIBLE. Whether you're sending an email, leaving a voicemail message, or engaging a member of the media directly through a phone conversation, always bring your A game. If you're lucky enough to get a reporter on the phone, be well rehearsed, to the point, and compelling. This means practicing or role-playing your pitch. If you decide to role-play, select a partner who will seriously challenge you. This will allow you to prepare for any number of questions the reporter might hurl your way. It may also calm your nerves, especially if the reporter or editor is brisk and attempts to rush you off the phone, which can be jarring, if not downright intimidating.

In addition to role-playing, I find writing my pitch helps keep me on track as it allows me to have critical points at the ready. If you decide to write your pitch, share it with a colleague to get his or her impression on whether it packs a punch or is filled with extraneous information. Reporters are typically jammed for time, so you'll want to quickly get to the point and then move on to the next person on your pitch list. In case it's not apparent, there is an important relationship between proactively pitching and planning. Proactive pitching requires advanced notice. You decrease your likelihood of success by calling a reporter the day—or even a couple days before—you want your story idea to appear in print. Give them enough notice to review your pitch and decide whether they will cover your news item. They also need time to pitch your concept to editors. A reporter may love your pitch on a protest involving singing grandmothers (such as those who joined the weekly Moral Monday protests in North Carolina in 2013) but forestall action on it if they don't have time to work it into their schedules or if current events present something more compelling.

As a rule of thumb, provide as much notice as possible. However, there are exceptions depending on your industry and the nature of the story you're pitching. If you are working on a political campaign or a union-organizing campaign and are planning an action, such as a press conference, picket, or rally, you want to notify the media on the day of the action or, in some cases, the night before. There's a reason for this approach. What you're trying to avoid here is tipping your hand and informing your opponent of your plans. For example, if you are planning a picket line outside of a company over the wages paid to workers, you'll want to advise the press the day of the event. Remember, once you send the advisory, the reporter may call the opposing entity to gain their thoughts in an effort to provide balance, or two sides to the news story. The company may ask the reporter to share your press advisory or release, thereby detailing all of your plans. I've had press releases I've sent to the media shared with the opposing party, and I've received press releases from employers and opposing entities simply by asking the reporter nicely. They usually oblige such requests. A good media relations person will always ask to see the opposing group's press release if the action or report in question targets their organization.

If I'm seeking a feature, I try to pitch the concept or idea four or five weeks in advance. This allows time to find the appropriate reporter for the story and allows them time to ponder the idea and then pitch an editor. Another benefit of pitching early is that it allows reporters time to possibly clear other items from their plate. Let's face it: Reporters are not sitting around waiting for story ideas. They have a portfolio of work and, assuming they deem it worthy, need to work your idea into their to-do list. With shrinking staff in newsrooms, it is imperative you plan early.

When pitching, focus on broad story ideas or concepts that have not previously been covered. Remember, many national media outlets, unlike local outlets, do not cover events. The *New York Times,* for instance, is unlikely to cover events. If it's not part of a broader trend or developing story, your chances of getting an event covered by the *New York Times* are slim to none. You will have to find a different angle. Remember, the job of the media is to report the news, not serve as an extension of your PR team. Prior to pitching a news outlet on an event you should have a good understanding of the circumstances that might make such an idea appealing.

BE RESPONSIVE. There also have been times when members of the media have sent highly confidential reports in exchange for my organization's candid feedback. Whenever a government entity releases a report, the media will look for feedback, good and bad, and may turn to advocates or industry leaders for input. It's difficult to offer meaningful and honest feedback without having had an opportunity to review the report in question. Reporters understand this and may share embargoed copies of reports and major policy announcements on the condition the source not disclose they received the information prior to the official release. This process helps members of the media with pre-reporting by ensuring they can file their story quickly after a report is released, rather than tracking down sources, waiting for them to read the documents in question, and then providing a response. Since reporters and producers are under a deadline to break the story as quickly as possible, try to be as responsive as possible. By the way, I'm not saying all reporters and producers follow this pre-reporting process, but many do.

The rule of not tipping your hand applies if you're in a communications role for a political campaign, government body, candidate, or a labor union working on an organizing campaign or negotiating a collective bargaining agreement. Aside from these exceptions, you cannot wait until the day of to pitch reporters. Give them a lead time of at least three or four days. If your item is a major issue, such as a closely watched trial or a rapidly escalating crisis, you may be allowed some wiggle room. As a general practice, however, aim to pitch (and re-pitch) reporters as early as possible. Remember, everyone has a boss, and reporters are no exception. Once you successfully pitch a reporter, giving them enough information to pique their interest, the reporter then must sell the story to their editor. You want to allow time for this process to run its course.

TACTIC 2
Develop and Use Your Network

I'm not a fan of waiting until I need a reporter to call them and ask them to cover a story. I want the reporter to know me and my organization before I even pick up the phone to make an ask. You don't always get this opportunity, but cultivating relationships with the media and potential sources is always the goal. As such, I work to build my network.

HOW TO DO IT

BE CREDIBLE. My network includes not just journalists, editors, producers, and media executives who cover or are interested in the topics my organization advocates, but also third-party validators who can attest to the claims of my organization on any number of issues. I also work to ensure my network includes "real people" or those impacted by the issues I'm advocating.

With respect to third-party validators, it's certainly easier to involve them in the story when they know and trust you. For example, it's much more powerful to identify youth who have been directly impacted by the school-to-prison pipeline than it is to offer only the media lawyers who can talk about the phenomenon. Both lawyers and impacted people are important. If my PR work focuses on education equity, such as school closures and overly harsh school disciplinary policies, my network should include people at all spectrums of the education continuum: educators, students, advocates, as well as juvenile justice reform advocates. I distinguish myself from other PR pros and advocacy groups when I can offer the media strong validators.

If you were a reporter, who would you trust: a communications director or a sitting judge? My vote is with the sitting judge. When thinking about your network, give thought to people whom the public deems trustworthy messengers. Teachers, nurses, judges, and students are examples of respected messengers. The extent to which you can combine your organizational leader with a trusted public messenger will maximize your media coverage. This is why a robust network is crucial for promoting your work or leader over the long term.

Just like members of the press, you should know these people before you enlist their help with something as significant as speaking to the media, as this can be intimidating. When you hear compelling stories, get to know the people behind the stories. Make a genuine effort to build a trusting relationship with them before you need them to advocate for you.

When I heard the story of honor student Kiera Wilmot, who had been suspended over a science project gone wrong, I asked one of the attorneys in my office at the time, Alana Greer, if she could get in touch with Wilmot's mother and her attorney. When Greer provided the contact information for the lawyer, I called him, introduced myself, and offered help sharing Kiera's story with the media; I was genuinely saddened by her experience and believe it was a classic example of the school-to-prison pipeline. The family attorney welcomed my call but asked me to touch base with Kiera's mom, Marie. After a series of conversations with Marie, I built a relationship with her and her daughter. They knew I was there to help rather than take from them. In this way, I planted the seeds for a long-term relationship that I still maintain to this day. Cultivating a relationship with sources and the media doesn't require a huge expenditure of resources. Even with a cash-strapped budget, it can yield outsized results.

BE CREATIVE. Reporters want the story. Never let the fact that you don't know the person you're pitching be a stumbling block for engaging them on a story idea. The first time I pitched Donna St. George of the *Washington Post*, I didn't know her. I saw that she covered education and thought she might be interested in Senator Dick Durbin's hearing on the school-to-prison pipeline, which I reference earlier in the book. Sometimes success has more to do with being bold than it does luck. The key is to try; and while you're at it, take some time to find a novel approach that will capture reporters' attention.

TACTIC 3
Develop Weekly Call/Pitch Lists

Each week, think about the reporters, editors, columnists, and media executives you want to contact and then develop a corresponding call list. Your list doesn't have to be incredibly long; just a few names will do. Of course, if you're planning a press event such as a media conference call, press conference, press briefing, or public gathering, you will automatically contact members of the media, if for no reason other than to ensure they know about your event. The concept of developing weekly call or pitch lists is for weeks when you have nothing planned. If you aim to do this every week, you may fall short, but not as short as if you had no goal in place at all.

The purpose of the weekly call/pitch list is to cultivate relationships with journalists and keep your organization on the radar. But keep in mind you must have something to say. You could share an article or blog post, give your media contacts a heads-up about a potential story, or invite them to coffee. To be clear, the call or pitch list is less about picking up an actual phone and more about initiating some form of contact, whether it's via the phone or email.

HOW TO DO IT

BE CREDIBLE. Every few weeks, I try to dedicate time to thinking about the work my organization is doing and studying which journalists are covering similar topics. I ask myself, "What is the media covering?" versus "What should they be covering?" I also think about which member of the media or which outlet might be most interested in the work my organization is doing. As I'm going through this thought process, I encourage others on my team to do the same thing.

For example, in thinking about restrictive voting laws and talking to members of my team, it occurred to me that many outlets were covering the mechanics of the various laws, but few were covering the hidden costs they incurred. I reasoned a story on the true cost of voter ID laws would be incredibly insightful. I thought about the reporters who might be interested in such a story and mapped a plan to pitch it.

BE RELENTLESS. For months I worked (albeit in vain) to get that article on the cost of voter ID laws placed. I was buoyed when the study, "The High Cost of 'Free' Photo Identification Cards," by Richard Sobel, was released in June 2014.[2] Sponsored by the Charles Hamilton Houston Institute for Race and Justice at Harvard Law School, the study affirmed what many intuitively believed, and it offered a mechanism for estimating the costs of so-called no-cost state IDs.

> The expenses for documentation, travel, and waiting time are significant, especially for minority-group and low-income voters—typically ranging from about $75 to $175. When legal fees are added to these numbers, the costs range as high as $1,500. Even when adjusted for inflation, these figures represent substantially greater costs than the $1.50 poll tax outlawed by the 24th amendment in 1964.

Doesn't this sound interesting? Like an article or feature begging to be written? I thought so too. I began pitching this concept in July 2014 to the *New York Times*, NBC's *Dateline*, and Nate Silver's *FiveThirtyEight* blog. Later that year (in October 2014) the Government Accountability Office (GAO) released a report titled, "Issues Related to State Voter Identification Laws," which offered empirical evidence that voter ID laws do indeed come at a cost for communities of color and lower-income families.[3] The GAO study received media coverage, which meant my desire to be the first person who brought the issue to the press, linking it to the work of my organization to challenge voter ID laws, had fallen short. However, I used the reports as an opportunity to share information with reporters on my weekly call list. So while I didn't actually place the story on the myth of "no-cost" IDs, I was able to share the information with my network of reporters.

Maintaining a call list obviously requires an investment of time. You cannot allow yourself to be so bogged down by the details that you miss the forest for the trees, as the cliché goes. PR pros must allow ourselves time and space to think a few steps down the line to what could and what should be covered.

BE CREATIVE. To assist in this forward-thinking process, I enlist as many thought partners as possible. During my team meetings, I encourage all team members to offer ideas for people we should be targeting in the press and stories we should be working to elevate. Since reporters will develop different types of relationships with different communicators, I try to learn who on my team has relationships with whom in the media and then determine the best person to do the outreach. In the end, we identify and plan outreach with far more reporters than one person could working alone.

TACTIC 4
Engage Editorial Boards

The primary responsibility of the editorial board is to publish editorials that represent the voice of the board and its publisher. The editorial board is separate from the newsroom and includes the Letters to the Editor and Opinion pages of a publication. While the editorial board is distinct from the newsroom, editorial page editors will sometimes invite reporters to participate in editorial board meetings, giving you the opportunity to potentially get your message into an editorial or a news article. There are four possible outcomes for every editorial board meeting:

- The paper can take a position in favor of your issue.
- The paper could write an editorial opposing your issue.
- The paper may elect to remain neutral and not weigh in at all.
- The news department could do an article explaining your position.

One of the benefits of editorial board meetings is that they can include more than just editorial board members. Sometimes the publisher of smaller outlets will attend editorial board meetings, and many editorial board editors also invite the reporter who covers the topic that you are discussing.

This partly explains why editorial board meetings are on the record unless you explicitly request—and the paper agrees—to an off-the-record discussion. Once you've met an editorial board member, reporter, or publisher and impressed on them who you are and what you represent, it is usually more difficult for them to vilify you. While they may not agree with your position on every issue, a face-to-face meeting with editorial boards could neutralize the board or dissuade them from weighing in on an issue. I highly recommend them.

When thinking about strategies and tactics to promote your issue, organization, or grassroots campaign, engage the editorial boards of publications that are local or national. If an issue gains prominence, editorial boards often weigh in and issue their opinion on the topic. Moreover, policy makers and other leaders routinely peruse this section of the publications. Since there is always a chance an editorial board could weigh in on a major issue, wouldn't you like them to have your perspective in mind before crafting a piece that could influence how others view a topic that is important to you?

HOW TO DO IT

BE CREDIBLE. Assign someone on your team to research the editorial page editors for all the papers in the cities and states where you work. For instance, if your organization is based in Ohio, you'd include all the major and smaller newspapers in Ohio: the *Columbus Dispatch*, the *Plain Dealer*, the *Akron Beacon Journal*, the *Toledo Blade*, *Dayton Daily News*, *Youngstown Vindicator*, the *Cincinnati Enquirer*, et cetera. If you don't have sufficient staff to do this, use a summer intern or call the communications or journalism department at a local college or university and ask them if they have a student who can work with you on this project. If all else fails, do it yourself. Just take your time, and try to identify one editorial page editor per week.

Next, read the editorials the publication has written in the last several months. This will give you a sense of whether the paper skews conservative, liberal, or libertarian. If a paper is an opponent of the issues I am espousing, I may forgo an editorial board with them, and opt for an editorial board memo.[4] Alternatively, I'll do an editorial board meeting with the understanding that I am seeking solely to neutralize the paper, not change their mind.

After I've researched the paper and its views, I begin thinking about who to take with me to the meetings. I want a subject matter expert, the leader of my organization, and perhaps an impacted person. I try to limit the number of people involved in the editorial board meeting so as not to outnumber the media outlet's representatives. Part of being credible in this instance is taking the right people who can effectively answer the array of questions that may be lobbed your way.

Another part of being credible is ensuring the team that will participate in the editorial board meeting is fully prepared. At this point, I begin prepping the team for the types of questions they're likely to receive. I also develop a prep memo of the members of the editorial board, the paper's position on any range of issues, the messages I want to convey during the meeting, and controversial topics that could be raised in the discussion. From here, I begin engaging editorial boards to see who will meet with me and my group.

If I am arranging multiple editorial boards, I normally try to schedule the smaller and the most ideologically similar outlets first. I want to allow the members who are participating as much practice as possible before moving them on to larger or more hostile outlets.

BE RESPONSIVE. Follow-up is usually required after editorial boards. Sometimes you need to provide reports and supporting documentation to undergird the claims you've made. In other cases, you may need to connect editorial board members with third-party validators. In some instances, the editorial board editor may offer you the opportunity to submit a guest column on the topic you discussed in the meeting. In a lot of cases, an editorial page member or editor will call you to fact-check claims just before they publish an editorial on the topic you all discussed. Whatever the follow-up, it's critical to respond in a timely fashion, to be responsive.

TACTIC 5
Utilize Op-eds (Guest Columns)

Op-eds, or guest columns, provide an opportunity to offer unfiltered commentary on a given issue. They allow the writer to tell a story on his or her own terms. Once published, the essay can be promoted through various digital media outlets, including Facebook, Twitter, blogs, and websites, making it evergreen. Opinion essays can live on into perpetuity.

Crafting opinion pieces can be time consuming. In addition to writing and editing, the piece must be successfully pitched to media outlets one at a time. Even though this is a time-intensive process, opinion editorials are worth the effort. In 2014, I set a goal for my team at Advancement Project to write, edit, or place twenty-four opinion editorials per year. We surpassed this goal, placing forty-one essays in news outlets as wide-ranging as LatinaLista, CNN, the *Hill,* and *Essence* magazine. And in 2015, we more than met this goal and placed forty-two opinion essays in outlets across the country.

The beauty of opinion essays is they are unfiltered commentary. They also allow people who don't always have a voice to share their thoughts on any number of issues with the world. They can greatly boost an organization's or leader's brand and, further, assuming you have communications staff with writing skills, they can be prepared with little to no resources other than the time it takes to write and pitch them to news outlets. Opinion editorials are one of the few earned media tools and tactics that give you the same benefit of paid media. Another is promoting your work via digital and social media channels such as Snapchat, blogs, Twitter, Facebook, and Instagram. (See Chapter 6 on social media.)

HOW TO DO IT

BE CREATIVE. If you're going to write an opinion essay, be sure your guest column coincides with the news cycle, as this will make it easier to have the piece published. Think about upcoming news hooks, and craft your opinion essay using one of those hooks. This may mean writing your essay and then holding it until current events make it timely.

Additionally, to the extent possible, try to recruit impacted people to write their own opinion essays. This ensures an authentic and unique voice and perspective. For some people, writing is intimidating. I normally tell people I work with to get their thoughts on paper and then send them to me to edit. When this doesn't work, I've also met with people one on one and recorded them as they relayed their experience. Armed with their authentic voice, I can then craft an opinion essay using their words. The bottom line is you want to include the appropriate voice and lived experiences of the authors in opinion essays.

BE CREDIBLE. Once the essay is written, I read it carefully and think about the most appropriate publication. Some essays lend themselves to the *Washington Post* and others to the *Hill*. It just depends on the types of essays each publication publishes and the style of writing. It's important that once an essay is written, the communicator allows sufficient time to pitch different publications. It normally takes several tries before an essay is accepted for publication.

Practically speaking, opinion essays should be between 700 and 750 words. Some publications require shorter or longer submissions. Be sure to check the submission guidelines before submitting your opinion essay.

TACTIC 6
Maximize Digital Media

Many people are visual learners, preferring to grasp information through photos and videos. One of the reasons Rev. Barber's Moral Monday protests in North Carolina were so successful was his team's use and distribution of dynamic photos and videos. Many of the photos were taken by photographer Phil Fonville, who sometimes refuses payment for grassroots movement work. His work can be accessed at www.philfonville.com. Eric Preston of Fusion Films often travels with Rev. Barber, capturing videos of his sermons, speeches, press conferences, and other actions. Preston uploads the videos on YouTube and other social media channels ensuring wide distribution. For people who have not met Barber directly, watching the videos gives them a sense of his style, mission, and purpose. It can also give them the sense of being part of the movement even though they may live states away. The NC NAACP's use of videos and photos also points to a broader lesson: Capturing videos, photos, or news articles is just the beginning. Once you secure these items, it's time to promote and disseminate them through digital media platforms.

Once you've successfully pitched and placed a news feature or article, and the story has appeared in print or captured amazing video footage, you have an awesome opportunity to share the work with an even broader audience. Once an article appears in print, you should promote it via digital media, including posting it on your organizational website or blog, or on social media platforms such as LinkedIn, Twitter, or Facebook. Rather than scheduling a single tweet or post on Facebook, send out a series of well-timed and strategic postings. You should also share the article or video with colleagues, donors, and potential donors, people working in your issue area, and reporters and producers who have covered or may consider covering the given topic in the future. (For more on the importance of social media for communications, please see Chapter 6.)

HOW TO DO IT

BE CREATIVE. While there will always be a role for communicators who focus on traditional media, and certainly traditional communicators should learn basic digital media skills, there is no substitute for investing in digital media staff. When I say *digital media*, I am referring to websites, the Internet, email advocacy, as well as social media platforms such as Instagram, Twitter, Pinterest, LinkedIn, Facebook, and Medium. There are some people who are hardwired to appreciate digital media. These individuals are happy to investigate emerging trends and ensure your organization is prepared to maximize them. These are the people you want on your payroll.

I have had great success with hiring recent college graduates to support my organization's digital media needs. I then invest in them and get them the additional training they want and desire. Some of this comes through digital media coaching. For years, I've worked with Alan Rosenblatt (*Dr. DigiPol*) of turner4D to coach and further develop the digital media talent at my organizations. Other times, I've sent digital media staffers to workshops and conferences. I've also hosted free communications skillshares with noted public and digital media experts for communicators in the Washington, D.C., area. These workshops help to expand the skillsets of communicators and also provide networking opportunities for attendees.

BE RELENTLESS. Social media is exciting and engaging, but one must still be relentless when using it. Once you craft a blog post or succeed in having a guest column published, your work has just begun. For instance, after you've published a blog post or guest column, share it on Twitter, Facebook, and LinkedIn Pulse. You might also consider sharing your published piece on StumbleUpon, Reddit, GrowthHackers, or Quora. This expands the audience that receives your message and amplifies your campaign reach.

TACTIC 7
Recruit and Utilize Third-party Validators

No one cares what you say about yourself. However, people do care what others say about you, which is why third-party validation is so important. As a public relations professional, you have no credibility until you earn it. Most journalists think we're liars, anyway. Don't believe me? Among other findings in a recent report put out by digital firm D S Simon, Kevin Allen writes, "90 percent of digital journalists say a PR pro has lied to them. Sixty-eight percent say that PR pros lie to them 'sometimes,' and 20 percent say they've been lied to 'often.' "[5] While perception is not always consistent with reality, I share these statistics to illuminate the barriers PR pros may face. Understanding this point of view helps explain the significance of surrogates or third-party validators.

It is critically important to build a coterie of well-respected people, individuals with a large and loyal following, and those regarded as having the ability to influence others. Your list of third-party validators could include traditional movers and shakers like politicians, academics, CEOs of large enterprises, celebrities, and ministers with large congregations who are commercially known (think TD Jakes).

Increasingly, corporations and others are also relying on online influencers (e.g., YouTube personalities, bloggers) to help promote their organizations or issues. I've retained high-profile bloggers—namely Danielle Belton (*The Black Snob*) and Alan Rosenblatt (*Dr. DigiPol*)—to serve as members of my organizations' echo chamber helping to highlight key issues in the racial and social justice movements. In Vancouver, Jessica Thomas Cooke and Hilary Chan-Kent created Wanderlust Management to represent online influencers and handle their business affairs. Online influencers can be found by tracking people with large online followings, and then monitoring the issues they regularly post about to see if there is alignment with your organization.

HOW TO DO IT

BE CREDIBLE. As I mentioned earlier in the chapter, take time to develop relationships with third-party validators before you need them. One way to build relationships with third-party validators is to seek out academics and researchers who focus on your program areas. When you see reports or books that affirm your organization's position on a given issue, reach out to the author or writer to express your support. Slowly begin to build a relationship with them by requesting a meeting, sharing information, and learning more about their thought process and beliefs. They should also know you and your organization's positions on various issues.

As you're identifying surrogates and third-party validators, be careful to ensure they're credible. In the same way that your own credibility is important, you don't want surrogates who will do more harm than good. Your surrogates should assist in garnering favorable media coverage, not create a media crisis that you then need to resolve. As I write, I'm thinking of then president-elect Donald J. Trump's surrogate Mark Burns who allegedly exaggerated some of his professional accomplishments.[6] The South Carolina preacher claimed to have had a Bachelor of Science degree and to have served in the United States Army. Both claims turned out to be false. Just a few days prior to the allegations of exaggerated accomplishments, Burns allegedly posted a cartoon of Democratic presidential nominee Hillary Clinton in blackface.[7] Both incidents detracted attention from Trump's candidacy and created news stories that did not advance the candidate's message. While it's impossible to know everything a surrogate will or will not do, the key is to thoroughly vet a person's past before enlisting them as a surrogate.

The Burns example may be a little more dramatic than what you or I might experience. Shortly after the tragic Sandy

Hook Elementary School shooting in Newtown, Connecticut, in December 2012, I organized a media conference call for Advancement Project to urge parents, educators, and others to examine the unintended consequences of police in schools, including dramatic rises in school-based arrests, police officers becoming involved in minor disciplinary issues, and, in some cases, excessive use of force against students. We wanted a collection of well-respected speakers who could speak to the natural tendency to want to keep kids safe but also of the need to proceed with caution when deploying police in schools.

Obviously, in the aftermath of a crisis, time is of the essence when it comes to generating media attention to advance policy positions or organizational goals. In addition to responding to the crisis, we were preparing to release a joint report, "Police in Schools Are Not the Answer to the Newtown Shooting," from Advancement Project, the NAACP Legal Defense and Education Fund (NAACP LDF), Dignity in Schools, and the Alliance for Educational Justice. I didn't have a lot of time to identify speakers for the call. Some of the speakers—like Matt Cregor, who at the time worked for the NAACP Legal and Education Defense Fund; Damon Hewitt, who also worked for the NAACP LDF at the time; and students who'd had experience with police in schools—were people with whom my organization had worked closely. At least one speaker, Gregory Thomas, the former executive director of school safety for New York City Public Schools, was not.

Much to my surprise, during the media call, Thomas highlighted the benefits of police in schools. His message was different from the one we had discussed. Had we (read *I*) done a little more research, we would have been prepared for Thomas's nuanced position. The call reinforced for me the need to thoroughly vet sources and validators before including them in our work.

BE RELENTLESS. It is easy to focus on the day-to-day activities of your job without focusing on relationship building with not just journalists but also third-party validators. Being relentless in this context is about being intentional about building relationships, while also regularly assessing who in your organization has relationships with whom. You do not need to know everyone, but you should have a good sense of who in your organization has relationships with influencers—academics, faith leaders, and other people who could potentially support your work as third-party validators. Surveying your leadership team and the broader staff of your organization to get a sense of their professional and personal networks is essential. You don't need to be creepy to do this. As your organization releases reports and other communications, share them with your network and ask your colleagues to do the same. Go one step further and try to get a sense of who is in your colleagues' networks as this will help you identify potential surrogates.

TACTIC 8
Package the Story

Whatever your topic, when pitching you want to make it as easy as possible for the media to cover. Spare no effort in going out of your way to help the reporter, producer, or host to acquire the material they need to cover your issue. Come to the table with story ideas, third-party validators to bolster your assertions, and real people (as opposed to talking heads, such as public relations officials) who are willing to speak with the reporter or producer. For example, if you want to pitch a voting rights story that focuses on the impact new voting law changes have on voters, come to the table with a list of people (including their phone numbers and email addresses) who can speak to the adverse impact the policy will have on them. Obviously, you will want to speak with the would-be spokesperson first to ensure he is interested in sharing his story prior to disclosing his contact information to the media. You'll also want to have an analysis of the voting law changes, why they were introduced, and the corresponding impact, with research and supporting documentation, such as reports or policy briefs, to back up your claims. It doesn't hurt to also have academics and other experts who can attest to your point of view. If you get the reporter or producer on the hook to write or produce your desired story, you'll have people lined up to help make it a success. It's important to have this information and these sources already in mind and at the ready so if a reporter decides to write the article, you are not slowing the process to go out and find the sources who will help shape your article.

HOW TO DO IT

BE RELENTLESS. The communicator should see her job as making the life of journalists easier. This means coming to reporters and columnists with story ideas, the supporting research materials, and people who are willing and available to speak with reporters should they decide to do a story. This is an ongoing effort. You should consistently collect testimonials before you ever land a news story. You should also work diligently to build your Rolodex of people impacted by the various policies your organization supports before they're ever needed. Here's why. It takes time to earn the trust of people you are asking to share their stories with the media. A lot of people are reluctant and fearful of being interviewed. If they know and trust you, they will be more inclined to speak with a reporter you endorse. In instances where you are proactively pitching story ideas, it's best not to wait until you get a reporter on the hook to do the legwork of identifying spokespersons, as this will slow the process.

BE RESPONSIVE. Of course, there will be instances when you are reacting to a media request, in which the reporter, producer, or editor, may have a specific profile of a person in mind with whom they would like to speak for a story, and you may not have the benefit of being prepared in advance. Even if you are reacting to a specific request from the media, you can still act quickly and identify the appropriate spokesperson. The broader point is to go out of your way to help the reporter with pre-reporting needs. Doing this will help solidify your relationships with the press while also helping to ensure you are elevating the issues for which you are most passionate. You cannot maximize the moment without carefully preparing the story you'd like the media to report.

Tactic 9
Organize and Facilitate Engaging Events

Sometimes we need to create opportunities to tell our stories. Solely relying on press releases is insufficient. We also need to create events that allow us to elevate the issue or campaign for which we're working. Events also provide fuel for broadcast media; moving images can sometimes capture our stories in a compelling way that the written word cannot.

HOW TO DO IT

BE CREATIVE. Years ago, I worked for America Coming Together, a 527 created by Steve Rosenthal. America Coming Together was an independent expenditure campaign in support of John Kerry's presidential bid. At the time, White House Chief of Staff Andrew Card was coming to Columbus, Ohio, to campaign for George W. Bush. Our communications team wanted to use the opportunity to highlight what we saw as flawed policies of the Bush administration. As such, we created a six-foot-tall, fluorescent pink greeting card with a message for Washington. After first alerting the media of our plans, we took the greeting card and stood outside the Ohio Statehouse. Columbus's WBNS Channel 10 attended our press avail and captured footage of our protest. This was a visual opportunity to highlight our message, and it proved incredibly effective.

The key to successful media events is being creative in your approach. Ensure your event is visually appealing with aspects that beg to be covered. Other examples include press conferences at the site of demonstrations, petition delivery drops, and counter-protests.

BE CREDIBLE. If you're going to plan a media event, do your research and plan it at a time that increases the likelihood that the media will show up; avoid planning events that take place during the lunch or evening newscast, or on Friday afternoons. Please also remember that many media outlets are unwilling or unable to pay overtime for weekend events, unless those events are major or large in scope in terms of attendees. Generally, it is best to avoid weekend press events.

While tactics will invariably shift from organization to organization, I chose to highlight the nine tactics above because they can be universally applied regardless of the personality of your organization. But please don't think they are exhaustive. They are offered as a floor and not a ceiling to help jump-start your own thinking around using creativity, responsiveness, credibility, and relentlessness to elevate noteworthy campaigns.

Crisis Communications

It's pointless to have a conversation about successfully promoting your issue, organization, or grassroots campaign without a simultaneous discussion on the art of managing a crisis. If you spend any length of time performing communications and public relations work for a candidate, organization, or company, you are bound to experience a crisis or two. It is the price of existing. At our core, we make mistakes. And some of those mistakes cost us dearly.

Examples of a crisis include a natural disaster, an executive's sudden departure without a clear succession plan, a public official being caught in a lie, allegations of wrongdoing by a CEO, the leak of highly sensitive internal documents or video footage, or an embarrassing conflict of interest for an elected official. A crisis has the potential to derail an organization's mission, alienate donors and supporters, and tarnish the leader's or organization's image and public standing. While potentially debilitating, a crisis can be greatly exacerbated by the response. Often, the response to the crisis can determine whether it lives on in perpetuity or is quickly resolved.

For a fire to thrive it needs three elements: heat, oxygen, and fuel. A crisis is a figurative fire. When confronting a crisis, you want to zap the oxygen at the source to put an end to the problem. Below are eight steps to extinguish the fire and get your organization back on track to fulfilling its mission. You will note that the main principles in play in crisis management are being responsive and being credible; that's because it is your organization's reputation on the line, and the only way to protect it is to act swiftly and honestly.

STEP 1
Avert a Crisis before It Begins

There are usually telltale signs that an issue, if left unaddressed, could snowball. It is always better to directly confront it rather than allow it to escalate. If left unchecked, these issues have the potential of wreaking havoc not only on executives and leaders but also on the institutions they represent. Bob Filner, anyone?

Former San Diego Mayor Bob Filner resigned in 2013 after more than eighteen women came forward and accused him of sexual harassment.[1] At least one of the victims sued Filner, as well as the city of San Diego. I'm hard-pressed to believe no one knew of the former mayor's unwelcomed sexual advances before news of them spilled into the public domain prompting his dramatic fall from grace. Did anyone try to put a stop to the harassment or hold the longtime elected official accountable? Did the people around him deflect their gaze due to his status and position?

The victims of sexual harassment could have been spared, Filner could have saved himself public humiliation, and the City of San Diego could have saved precious resources, had he owned up to his behavior and sought help prior to being forced to do so. (Sources estimated the special election to replace him would cost anywhere from $3 million to $6 million.)

HOW TO DO IT

BE RESPONSIVE. Waiting until a crisis begins before you think through how you'll handle unforeseen problems is too late. Sure, there is no way to predict every possible crisis, but if you have a plan in place, you are better prepared to deal with the challenges that will come your way. Every organization should have a crisis communications plan that identifies the overall crisis management plan, protocols, and contact information for key leaders internal and external to the organization. Planning for a crisis means you've assembled a skilled internal team charged with thinking through policies for handling difficult situations. The crisis management team could include legal counsel, the senior communications team, the management or leadership team, as well as the organization's executive director. You might also consider people in non-management positions to ensure diversity of thought and experience.

STEP 2

Outline Your Goals and Objectives

No one plans to have a crisis, and when they occur, they usually come on suddenly. Prior to setting out on any communications task, public relations professionals should first identify the overarching goal. In my experience, controlling the narrative, shifting from defense to offense, and working to regain the trust of your constituents are often the main goals when dealing with a crisis.

HOW TO DO IT

BE CREDIBLE. Suppose you're left in the unenviable position of controlling your narrative while also dealing with the problem at hand. While this is difficult, it can be done; however, you must be disciplined about using the narrative your team has developed. The narrative should include your organization's and leader's values, principles, and mission statement. You'll want to outline a specific statement for the issue at hand, recite the statement, and then pivot back to the broader narrative. This will help you to frame the issue in the most beneficial light.

Be creative. Next, you want to shift from defense to offense. With jarring revelations, you're often left scrambling, though you must address the crisis at hand. Then you can think strategically about ways to move to offense, where you're no longer responding but working to help your company regain the trust of employees, board members, clients, and the public. One way to shift from the defense to the offense is to strategically engage surrogates to speak on your behalf. Another way to move to a more favorable position is to announce a major report, policy initiative, or campaign that would shift the focus from the undesirable issue to one that allows you and your organization to shine.

STEP 3
Tell the Truth and Apologize

Few things are as frustrating as feeling one is being purposely misled, and nothing sinks credibility faster than being caught in a lie. It's best to tell the whole truth—and nothing but the truth—prior to being forced to do so. A refusal to be honest only fuels the story, keeping it alive in the media day after day. Explain the situation as best you can; tell the truth and apologize. Once you've done that, the story's shelf life is significantly reduced.

HOW TO DO IT

BE CREDIBLE. Lay out the situation on your own terms. Put it out there and give people an opportunity to process it. It will be embarrassing and it may be painful, but being honest is almost always the best course of action. Think about the revelations involving former Baltimore Ravens player Ray Rice, who was found to have pummeled his then fiancée Janay Palmer in an Atlantic City, New Jersey, casino. In February 2014, TMZ leaked a video showing the Ravens' star player dragging Palmer's seemingly lifeless body out of an elevator. While many speculated Palmer was the victim of domestic violence, those fears were confirmed when TMZ released yet another video showing the muscular Rice knocking Palmer unconscious, then standing over her with seeming little concern for her well-being. The release of the videos left fans reeling and wondering why a more severe punishment was not meted out—Rice initially received a two-game suspension following the release of the first video. When the public sensed a cover-up, embattled NFL Commissioner Roger Goodell's public image deteriorated. There were repeated calls for his ouster. While Ray Rice abusing his wife was troubling in and of itself, the NFL's handling of the situation created an unnecessary PR disaster. Now there were at least two competing narratives in the media: the domestic violence involving Rice and other NFL players, and a potential cover-up by Goodell and the league.

I would have advised both Rice and the NFL to immediately come clean, apologize for being untruthful and failing to adequately address domestic violence. From there, I would have urged the NFL to outline an aggressive plan to address domestic violence. I might also have recommended the impaneling of a watchdog agency or entity to steward the culture change.

BE RESPONSIVE. If you've ever witnessed an irate customer voicing his frustrations to a store manager or employee, you know it's quite a sight. If you've ever been on the receiving end of such a call or encounter from a highly annoyed client or customer, you know how tense the situation can be and how delicately the conversation must be handled. You know that often the best way to diffuse the situation is to apologize.

When someone has been wronged, there is a natural desire for vindication, to experience some form of justice. It is often hard to forgive without recompense. There must be an attempt to right the wrongs. Kathleen Griffin, the author of *The Forgiveness Formula: How to Let Go of Your Pain and Move On with Life*, echoed this sentiment:

> Children naturally have a strong sense of justice. They will often protest that an adult decision "is not fair.". . . This sense of natural justice is a good starting place to teach children that they can deal with arguments in a way that leaves both sides feeling satisfied, and the most important key to that is for both of them to be heard. This idea of "things being put right" is central to justice and the possibility of forgiveness. This is something we need to learn early as children.[2]

In disagreements or when problems arise, people want two things: an opportunity to be sufficiently heard and an apology. If you or your organization has made a mistake, you owe your customers or client base an apology, as well as space to appropriately voice concerns and grievances. Don't make excuses. And for the love of all things right, do not offer half-hearted or obscure apologies. An apology should always be sincere, not a shallow tactic to evade the public's gaze. You've seen elected officials, celebrities, and media personalities fumbling over themselves to offer half-apologies for misdoings or offensive remarks. This is patronizing and self-defeating. Be sincere and offer an unequivocal apology.

STEP 4

Beware of the Drip . . . Drip . . . Drip

The danger of not disclosing the whole truth is the constant drip of new information and seedy details about what has been said or done. Your organization will take a beating with each new revelation. The constant drip, drip, drip of new details will give the story oxygen and keep it alive. Think back to the earlier example of the NFL Ray Rice scandal. While Goodell maintained his innocence, there was a steady drip of news articles and media reports suggesting his complicity in hiding the initial video or incompetence in failing to obtain it. The situation was handled poorly.

HOW TO DO IT

BE RESPONSIVE. Deal with issues or problems in one fell swoop. Otherwise you will get stuck in a tiresome yo-yo game, forced to react and respond as new details are divulged. Parsing out details piecemeal creates credibility issues, which can create a tiresome loop for your employees, board, customers, and other supporters. Sometimes it can even be helpful to pre-emptively release damaging information before someone else has an opportunity to do so.

STEP 5

Seek Professional Help

There is no shame in seeking help. Depending on the crisis, it may be wise to bring in outside counsel. Bringing in outside communications assistance to help during a crisis may be costly. However, how one manages a crisis will have long-term implications for the viability and reputation of your brand. If you don't handle a crisis appropriately, you may not have an organization in the long run.

So there are multiple benefits of paying for crisis communications assistance. First, these are people who devote each day to handling sensitive matters with diplomacy and control. Public relations firms that focus on crisis communications are experts at managing difficult situations in a manner that preserves a leader's legacy and an institution's public standing, as well as resolving the issue at hand. When jarring things happen to organizations it's easy to become stuck and immobilized with fear and concern. Bringing in outside help, someone who is not readily attached to the crisis and can be objective, is often very productive.

Have you ever attempted to do something on your own, only to find out after repeated tries that you would have been better off asking for help? Think about the person who believes he can fix anything but lacks the know-how to do so. Playing with wires and taking on housing repairs could end disastrously. Don't be that guy. Ask for help. Don't wait until a situation spirals out of control to request assistance. By that point, it may be too late. Do yourself a favor and seek help early. If you are faced with an unexpected crisis, and you, as well as the management team of your organization, believe you may benefit from extra help, immediately work to seek out help.

HOW TO DO IT

BE RESPONSIVE. How do you know when you're in over your head? Ask yourself this question: is a new perspective and approach needed? Also, consider how empowered your current PR team is to make decisions, take over day-to-day operations, and map the plan to resolve the crisis. The less empowered you are, the more important getting outside counsel will be to move your organization back into the public's trust.

Every section of this book is important. However, the crisis communications section is the insurance policy for your work. You could work like hell to build solid relationships with the press that generate favorable media coverage for your organization yet be undone due to an unexpected crisis. In the same way you wouldn't purchase a home or car without insurance, take special care to insure your hard work by developing a crisis management plan before you need it. This enables you to respond to a crisis with confidence. The other benefit of outlining a crisis management plan and communicating it with your team before a crisis hits is that you may not have the time or clarity of thought to do this once you're in the thick of things. And remember, even though you have a crisis management plan in place, don't be afraid to seek professional help if you believe the crisis is outside the realm of what you're able to comfortably handle.

CONCLUSION

Leading in the Midst of Fear
Using the Four Principles

You may ask what leading in the midst of fear has to do with communications and public relations. Everything.

In our line of work, we hear no more than yes. It's very easy to internalize no and make a judgment about your capabilities and skillset. And with a history of nos, it's tempting to develop debilitating fear.

There are many resources to help one lead in the midst of fear. One of my favorites is Arianna Huffington's *On Becoming Fearless*.[1] It covers every aspect of overcoming fear from aging and rearing children to managing a career and pursuing one's dreams. This book is especially pertinent for women who, according to the Bureau of Labor Statistics, make up 63 percent of public relations professionals.[2] Huffington writes:

> Sure, nobody likes to fail, but in many women the fear of
> failure translates into taking fewer risks and not reaching for
> our dreams. And the fear of not living up to some mythical

ideal of perfection often means that many of us won't move ahead with a project or idea until we are 110 percent sure it's perfect, error-free, and unassailable. Which often means never moving ahead, or not moving as far or as fast as we could.

The Confidence Code by Katty Kay and Claire Shipman holds more valuable lessons on leading through fear.[3] Among other things, the book describes the fallacy in waiting for perfection prior to moving on one's objectives and plans. It is geared specifically to women, or men seeking a better understanding of women, and has been incredibly helpful in shedding light on things that sometimes hold female leaders back. (Hint: our perception of our own capabilities and the relentless pursuit of perfection is a huge factor in what holds us back.) Shipman and Kay remind us that "the people who succeed aren't always naturals. They are doers."

Fearlessness is imperative for successfully promoting an issue or cause. At a minimum, communicators must learn to feel the fear and proceed anyway. One of the ways that I keep that fear in check is by asking questions—lots of them. In his May 29, 2014, column for *Forbes*, contributor Jayson DeMers listed, "7 Things Good Communicators Always Do."[4] Numbers four and five focus on asking questions, both to ensure you understand your audience and to receive the clarification necessary to effectively communicate.

Over time, I learned that asking questions is the best way to improve and grow. If I pitch an opinion piece, and the opinion page editor declines my submission, I will gently ask the reason for the decision. Sometimes they will share their rationale, as was the case with my team's submission to the *Washington Post* on the Washington football team name. It turned out the piece was submitted too close to the desired publication date. If I had not inquired about their reasoning, I would have missed critical information on how to successfully place guest columns in the future.

I appreciate the importance of asking why. Why did one plan work and another did not? Why is this the best course of action for this moment in time? Why did an outlet decline to publish my guest column? Why did one press release get picked up and another did not? I learned that if I do not ask why, it's far too easy to develop a negative perception of my abilities when there could be broader contextual information that led to the negative outcome.

For instance, I planned a media conference call to discuss the work my organization was doing around voting rights in North Carolina. I'd orchestrated numerous successful calls, and I was sure this latest call would go off without a hitch. The call was held at 11 a.m. on a Monday. I know what you're thinking: horrible day for a press call, right? I should have known. As you may have guessed, very few reporters joined the call and I was beyond disappointed. I had two options: Write it off as a failed media call or think about ways to increase the likelihood of success on future calls. I opted to evaluate what went wrong and determine how to prevent similar problems in the future.

The problem was clear. Barring a major announcement or hot-button issue, calling a reporter on the day of an event is like eating a whole cake in one sitting and begging to lose weight. It doesn't work. Ultimately, our media call suffered because we didn't have enough lead time to pitch and re-pitch reporters. In addition, Monday morning media calls are particularly difficult. Reporters are returning to work following a weekend and no doubt preparing for the week ahead. They're being pitched by scores of public relations professionals, and a Monday morning call is probably the last thing on their minds.

Jeffrey J. Fox said it best in his book *How to Become CEO*:

Mistakes are milestones. They indicate action in new and unexpected areas. They are learning devices. Whatever the root cause of your mistake, record it. You probably will never make it again. Make notes on what you learned, how you would handle the same event again. Acknowledging mistakes is a sign of security and confidence. . . . A record of mistakes is often the memorabilia of a very successful person.[5]

Sometimes even the best laid plans go awry. And other times, things go well when they could have gone great. The best way to improve is to constantly ask yourself and others how a campaign or event went. Feedback should also include what you or your team could have done differently. Ask what went wrong and why. I also suggest conducting debriefs and evaluations after every event or campaign. And in the case of written materials, share the piece with multiple people prior to submitting it to gain varied perspectives. Asking questions is the best hope for improving outcomes and countering fear. What is more, it is essential to applying the four principles of extraordinary PR on an ordinary budget: being credible, creative, responsive, and relentless.

Feed the Spirit

If you feel you are barely treading water in terms of promoting the work your organization is doing, you may rightly wonder how to keep moving in the face of disappointments that will inevitably come. In addition to asking questions that will inform your future success, the key is to feed your spirit. Due to the high propensity of burnout, identifying your own source of inspiration is critical to long-term success in public relations. Each of us is wired differently, however, so finding things that motivate and bring immense joy will vary depending on the person.

Public relations professionals are always on the clock. We receive nonstop information and are charged with distilling it into more usable forms. We are often responsible for haranguing the press while meeting other organizational demands. Even when we're not technically working, a crisis could push us into working evenings, weekends, and even holidays. Alternatively, a reporter may reach out to us on the weekend and need an immediate response. Since we work with journalists who are often under deadlines, we too work under tight deadlines. It's no wonder then that in September 2015, CareerCast listed careers in public relations, a major component of communications, among the top ten most stressful professions behind jobs in the military and public safety.[6]

One of the ways to ensure you're able to work in public relations and communications over the long haul is by being intentional about finding aspects of your job that feed your spirit. For me, I love bringing people together by organizing and hosting impactful communications events. During the day, I'm charged with writing pitch notes and editing press releases and opinion pieces, but during the evenings and on weekends, I bring people together to discuss various issues in communications and racial justice. This is inspiring beyond belief. I get a kick out of organizing highly engaging panel presentations that provide space to dialogue about issues of race.

The other thing that feeds my spirit and has enabled me to have a long career in public relations is setting and reaching seemingly unattainable goals where communications is concerned. Few things give me more joy than setting my sights high, mapping the plan to reach those goals, and then ultimately succeeding. And even if I don't succeed, I learn valuable lessons in the process. So for me, finding the joy has been about being strategic in thinking through how to sustain my enthusiasm and commitment to communications over the long term.

One of my former team members, Jumoke Balogun, was pitching a news story on the difficulties young LGBTQ students of color have in schools across the country. Most people have no concept of the double stigma of race and sexual orientation that these students face. To make schools more inclusive, it is critical to collect and share stories about the experiences of LGBTQ youth. Included in Balogun's pitch list was the seemingly unattainable MTV. I was over-the-moon excited when I learned that she not only captured the media outlet's attention but convinced them to cover the story. This ensured that a broader audience beyond racial justice or LGBTQ reporters and activists got to learn about the experiences of LGBTQ youth of color. Imagine how these youth, who sometimes feel forgotten and overlooked, must have felt upon reading the MTV story. This was the sort of soaring victory that propels communicators to continue setting and achieving lofty goals.

An example of my feeding my own spirit was when I helped to get Rev. Dr. Barber on HBO's *Real Time with Bill Maher* in the summer of 2014.[7] Less than two months after the first Moral Monday protest and our round-the-clock media work, Bill Maher's booking agent reached out. Once she reached out, I stored her contact information, vowing to pitch and re-pitch the Forward Together Movement that organized Moral Mondays until Barber was on the show. In practical terms, this meant sending monthly or bimonthly notes to the booking agent detailing Barber's work. It bears mentioning that I rarely received a response to the emails. It felt like I was sending messages into a dark hole—but I wasn't receiving a failure notice, so I knew my messages were landing. After two rejections and more than a year had passed, Rev. Barber was booked to appear on the show.

The appearance was important because it allowed Rev. Barber to deliver his message of urging the North Carolina state legislature to govern based on our deepest moral values to a broad demographic.

Our movement needs public relations professionals who

are in it for the long haul. From eligible voters being blocked from the ballot box to retail employees struggling to provide basic sustenance for their families due to low wages and poor working conditions, the disconcerting effects of climate change, and the millions of aspiring Americans seeking a fair pathway to legal status in the United States, our nation is crying for justice. When eligible voters are forced to make ten trips to the Department of Motor Vehicles and other state offices, drive more than 200 miles and spend more than twenty hours in order to obtain a voter ID, as ninety-four-year-old Rosanell Eaton of North Carolina was forced to do, we know the very essence of our democracy is in peril. When you consider the almost ritualistic headlines of scores of unarmed African American men, boys, women, and girls assaulted or killed by those charged to protect and serve, it's easy to lose hope. That is why feeding the spirit is more than a fuzzy moniker.

While the nation is indeed hurting, we are in a pivotal moment. This moment can ill afford bystanders. Everyone has a role to play, and there are many tools we can embrace to accomplish our goals. Of all the tools in the arsenal, communications is a standout. Communications can play a pivotal role in provoking dialogue and creating public will for change and reform. Were it not for the advent of social media, where anyone can record and upload videos capturing the treatment of ordinary Americans, many injustices would go unacknowledged. Were it not for the twenty-four-hour news cycle and the communicators and institutions that feed them, innumerable issues would occur outside the watchful public eye. Were it not for organizations using communications to demonstrate their value and ability to facilitate change, they would lack critical funding to carry out groundbreaking work. For these reasons and more I am increasingly hopeful of the prospect for change and the ability of public relations and communications to help usher in that change.

In this book, I've outlined a series of principles that will assist communicators in elevating the work of their organizations. I know it's easy for me to offer these recommendations without knowing the details of your work situation—how many communicators are on your team, the skill level of your internal communications department, the budget, et cetera—but the principles really do apply regardless of what you're promoting and what your budget is. And they are especially impactful when they're layered together.

The four principles—being credible, creative, responsive, and relentless—are what help you maximize media coverage. Media credits directly correspond to an organization's brand, which in turn has an impact on funding for nonprofits and revenue for those in the private sector. Media coverage is the means to promote your organization, generate interest and support of donors, hold elected officials or employers accountable, or to build a grassroots movement or campaign.

Understanding the importance of being creative to generate media interest or responsive when you engage the media is critical whether you're working on a political campaign, for an organization, or on an issue advocacy campaign. Understanding how being credible sets you up for mutually beneficial relations with the media will pay dividends for both your professional career as well as your organization's brand. Being relentless is the key to long-term success in public relations, where you can hear no ten times before you get a yes, and again means that you guarantee that the work of your organization will be successfully highlighted in the media and in the court of public opinion.

Learning how to diplomatically request a correction to a news story, so as not to cause long-term damage in a relationship with a reporter, is relevant whether you're part of a grassroots movement or leading communications for a business official or a school board candidate These principles are the prerequisites to enjoying extraordinary PR on an ordinary budget.

I have learned and used these principles over the course of my career in communications and public relations to great success. I want you to be successful too. That's why I encourage you to combine lessons from your practical experience with the recommendations outlined in this book to increase your value to your organization and to the broader movement you are working to support. As you reflect on your own experiences and work to always be credible, creative, responsive, and relentless, I know you will experience extraordinary PR on an ordinary budget.

ACKNOWLEDGMENTS

Prior to moving forward, I want to acknowledge a key source of my inspiration: my beautiful son, Cameron Blackwell. In more ways than one, Cameron is my hero. In writing this book, I hope to leave him a legacy of appreciation for language and advocacy.

I also extend my thanks to my family and close friends, including my parents, siblings David and Sabrina Farmer, and dear friends Phyllis Quartey-Ampofo, Melany J. Silas, Amy Lambrecht, Teresa Todd, Amanda Hoyt, Bill and Teri Pritchett, and Margot Friedman. I also thank a host of mentors, including Jolene Molitoris, former Ohio State senator Nina Turner, and Gerry Hudson. Thank you to Daniel Giosta, who on several occasions reviewed and edited my work; key members of my current and prior team, including Chelsea Fuller, Jumoke Balogun, Ricardo Ramirez, Andrew Ambrogi, Jeralyn Cave, Victoria Wenger, and Cynthia Gordy; and Shuya Ohno, who listened with great interest to my book idea and then introduced me to his friend, Gayatri Patnaik, executive editor at Beacon Press. Patnaik read my work in its early stages and helped me think through the best approach for sharing it with the world. I also express gratitude to my editor Anna Leinberger, who worked with me for over a year and a half on this book. There would be no *Extraordinary PR* without her. Thank you to the wonderful staff of PICO National Network; Advancement Project's current and former staff and partners, including Penda D. Hair, Judith Browne Dianis, Edward A. Hailes, Pam and Ricardo Martinez, Evelin Urrutia, and Ingris Moran. Finally I also express deep appreciation to the Reverend Dr. William J. Barber II and attorney Al McSurely of the North Carolina NAACP.

GLOSSARY

CALL LIST: A list of reporters, producers or hosts you intend to contact on any variety of news stories.

COMMUNICATOR: A communications or public relations practitioner; someone whose sole job is communications.

CRISIS: For the purposes of this book, a crisis is defined as any situation with the potential to derail an organization's or company's mission, alienate donors and supporters, or tarnish a leader's or organization's image and public standing.

DIGITAL MEDIA: Any media that is coded in a machine-readable format. It encompasses websites as well as social media platforms such as Twitter, Facebook, YouTube, LinkedIn, Pinterest, and Instagram.

EARNED MEDIA: Media coverage that has not been purchased. Examples include television or radio appearances, opinion editorials (or guest columns), letters to the editor, blog posts, as well as print and online articles. While earned media doesn't require a financial outlay—other than the time of the communications professional—it is subject to commentary from reporters and editors and, therefore, not as controlled as paid media. What do I mean by *controlled*? If you purchase a series of radio or television ads (paid media), the ads will feature only your chosen words, not those added by a network or others.

EMBARGO: An agreement to share information with the media with the understanding that it will be shared publicly only after an agreed-upon date. It allows reporters time to do background reporting on a given topic.

EVERGREEN CONTENT: Content that retains its value and doesn't easily disappear; once it's published, it can be accessed again and again.

NEWS HOOK: Something that captures the media's attention or coincides with current events. It is the reason for covering an issue at a given point in time.

OFF THE RECORD: Refers to remarks offered on a story or media report that may be used in a story but not attributed to the source. The information shared is usually confidential, and the reporter or media representative must agree to go "off the record" to allow a source to share the confidential or sensitive information.

OPINION EDITORIAL (AKA OP-ED OR GUEST COLUMN): Opinion editorials run opposite a newspaper's editorial page or appear in the opinion section of a media outlet's website. The opinion editorial represents the views of an external person or entity, rather than an editorial, which represents the views of the media outlet's publisher. Opinion editorials are typically 750 to 800 words in length.

PACKAGE THE STORY: To provide all the information a reporter or producer might need to report or cover a given issue. It includes providing additional sources and their contact information. It also includes providing contextual information to ensure the story is covered from the desirable perspective or angle. Packaging the story might also include embargoed copies of reports or policy papers, which allow the reporter or producer to preview the material in order to write a story about it.

PAID MEDIA: As the name implies, paid media is media that is purchased. Paid media is desirable because it allows for a controlled message, whereas a news article, for example, is subject to a reporter's or editor's interpretation and influence.

PITCH: To sell a concept or idea to media executives, producers, reporters, and editors. Pitching usually refers to the process of encouraging the media to cover a particular story or idea. It is essentially a sales proposal focused on selling a given story idea.

PITCH LIST: A list of reporters you are pitching on a given topic. The pitch list includes the names of the reporters, their corresponding media outlet, and their contact information.

PLACE: To successfully plant a story idea, which a media outlet then covers via a written article or TV segment.

SEGMENT: TV programs are broken into segments, which allows the show to focus on different issues during a given broadcast. A segment is a portion of a TV show dedicated to a given issue.

STRATEGIC COMMUNICATIONS: Focuses on utilizing communications to achieve a strategic goal or objective. It is a system of constant evaluation to strategically determine the best approach to solve or address a given problem.

SURROGATE: Someone authorized to speak on behalf of someone else. A surrogate usually comes to the aid of leaders or media executives by speaking favorably on their behalf. Surrogates also explain the thinking or rationale of a leader.

THIRD-PARTY VALIDATION: Support of an angle or point by an external entity. For instance, assuming a federal judge or similarly situated elected official affirms the policy position of a given organization, the affirmation by the external and respected leader can be said to be a form of third-party validation.

TRADITIONAL MEDIA: Print, radio, and TV media outlets.

NOTES

PREFACE

1. Guy Kawasaki, "The Art of Evangelism," GuyKawasaki.com, January 12, 2006.

2. Betsy Woodruff, "A Kinder, Gentler Scott Walker," *Slate*, November 4, 2014, http://www.slate.com/articles/news_and_politics/politics/2014/11/scott_walker_s_closing_argument_in_wisconsin_is_a_soft_one_the_conservative.html.

3. SAG-AFTRA, "Tony Shalhoub, Susan Sarandon Fire up Wisconsin Protesters," March 14, 2011, https://www.sagaftra.org/tony-shalhoub-susan-sarandon-fire-wisconsin-protesters (accessed September 14, 2016).

ONE

1. Jennifer Bendery, "Rashad Robinson Is Leading the Social Justice Movement into the 21st Century," Huffington Post, May 6, 2015.

2. Dustin Volz, "AOL Becomes the Latest Tech Giant to Flee from ALEC," *The National Journal*, November 10, 2014, https://www.nationaljournal.com/s/35635/aol-becomes-latest-tech-giant-flee-from-alec.

3. While the assistor language was defeated during the 2013 Florida legislative session, it was reintroduced in 2015 as part of a broader restrictive voting measure.

4. It bears noting that Rev. Dr. Barber and the North Carolina State Conference of the NAACP had been organizing and working in North

Carolina for at least 7 years prior to the start of the weekly Moral Monday protests. To be fair, "Moral Mondays" grew out of a 7-year movement, before Advancement Project was ever involved. On their own, the NC NAACP generated tremendous regional media coverage. My contribution, once I began working with the NC NAACP in 2013, was to expand that media coverage, particularly among national media outlets.

5. Sally Stewart, *A Guide to Meeting the Press: Media Training 101* (Hoboken, N.J.: John Wiley & Sons, Inc., 2004), 19.

6. U.S. Department of State, "The Decline of Union Power," About.com, http://economics.about.com/od/laborinamerica/a/union_decline.htm (accessed September 12, 2016).

TWO

1. Daniel J. Losen and Tia Elena Martinez, "Out of School & Off Track: The Overuse of Suspensions in American Middle and High Schools," Report, The Civil Rights Project's Center for Civil Rights Remedies, April 8, 2013, https://civilrightsproject.ucla.edu/resources/projects/center-for-civil-rights-remedies/school-to-prison-folder/federal-reports/out-of-school-and-off-track-the-overuse-of-suspensions-in-american-middle-and-high-schools/Exec_Sum_OutofSchool_OffTrack_UCLA.pdf (accessed September 12, 2016).

2. Youtube video, "How a Science Project Got a Student Arrested," advancementproject.org, May 29, 2014, https://www.youtube.com/watch?v=cX8l7FTyHgM (accessed September 12, 2016).

THREE

1. Michael Alison Chandler, "Alexandria Students Push for Alternatives to Suspensions," *Washington Post*, January 5, 2014, https://www.washingtonpost.com/local/education/alexandria-students-push-for-alternatives-to-suspension/2014/01/05/c4c520c4-7491-11e3-8b3f-b1666705ca3b_story.html (accessed September 14, 2016); Moriah Balingit, "Civil Rights Advocates Slam Alexandria School System over Discipline Data," *Washington Post*, June 13, 2016, https://www.washingtonpost.com/local/education/civil-rights-advocates-slam-school-system-over-discipline-data/2016/06/13/91239ae2-3182-11e6-95c0-2a6873031302_story.html (accessed September 14, 2016).

2. Advancement Project, "Barriers to the Ballot in 2016," July 2016,

http://www.advancementproject.org/blog/entry/infographic-barriers-to-the-ballot-restrictive-voting-procedures-in-2016 (accessed September 14, 2016).

3. Roy Greenslade, "PRs Outnumber Journalists in the US by a Ratio of 4.6 to 1," *Guardian*, April 14, 2014, https://www.theguardian.com/media/greenslade/2014/apr/14/marketingandpr-usa (accessed September 14, 2016).

4. Keith Ferrazi with Tahl Raz, *Never Eat Alone: And Other Secrets to Success, One Relationship at a Time* (New York: Crown Publishing Group, 2005).

5. Jeffrey J. Fox, *How to Become CEO: The Rules for Rising to the Top of Any Organization* (New York: Hyperion, 1998), 56.

6. Moe Foner, *Not for Bread Alone* (Ithaca: Cornell University, 2002), 98–99.

7. Race Forward, Clocking In, https://clockingin.raceforward.org/ (accessed September 14, 2016).

FIVE

1. Donna St. George, "'School-to-Prison' Pipeline Hearing Puts Spotlight on School Discipline," *Washington Post*, December 13, 2012, https://www.washingtonpost.com/local/education/school-to-prison-pipeline-hearing-puts-spotlight-on-student-discipline/2012/12/13/18503286-4524-11e2-9648-a2c323a991d6_story.html (accessed September 18, 2016).

2. Donna St. George, "A Shift in Denver: Limits on Police in Schools," *Washington Post*, February 18, 2013, https://www.washingtonpost.com/local/education/a-shift-in-denver-limits-on-police-in-schools/2013/02/18/932083b4-791b-11e2-9a75-dab0201670da_story.html (accessed September 18, 2016).

3. Penda D. Hair, "This Football Season, Let's Wipe 'Redskins' from our Vocabulary," MSNBC.com, September 14, 2014, http://www.msnbc.com/msnbc/football-season-lets-wipe-redskins-our-vocabulary (September 18, 2016).

4. Richard Wolf, "Voting Rights Cases May Be Heading Back to Supreme Court," *USA Today*, September 11, 2014, http://www.usatoday.com/story/news/nation/2014/09/11/voting-rights-states-courts-wisconsin-texas-north-carolina-ohio/15279621/ (accessed September 18, 2016).

SIX

1. "Here's How Many People Are on Facebook, Instagram, Twitter and Other Big Social Networks," *Adweek*, April 4, 2016, http://www .adweek.com/socialtimes/heres-how-many-people-are-on-facebook -instagram-twitter-other-big-social-networks/637205 (accessed December 19, 2016).

2. Zephora, "The Top 20 Valuable Facebook Statistics—Updated February 2017," https://zephoria.com/top-15-valuable-facebook-statistics/.

3. *Adweek*, 2016.

4. Jackie Borchardt, "Ohio Education Department Spokesman Apologizes for Tweet Suggesting Critics Should 'Get Laid,'" Cleveland. com, July 24, 2014, http://www.cleveland.com/open/index.ssf/2014/07/ ohio_education_department_spok.html (accessed December 19, 2016).

5. Laura Stampler, "DiGiorno Used a Hashtag about Domestic Violence to Sell Pizza," *Time*, September 9, 2014, http://time.com/ 3308861/digiorno-social-media-pizza/ (accessed on December 19, 2016).

6. Jennifer Farmer, "Bree Took a Stand. Will You?" *HuffingtonPost*, June 29, 2015, http://www.huffingtonpost.com/jennifer-farmer/bree -took-a-stand-will-you_b_7688888.html (accessed December 19, 2016).

SEVEN

1. Lou Hoffman, "The Evolving Distribution and Role of Press Releases," *Ragan's PR Daily*, August 10, 2014, http://www.prdaily.com/ mediarelations/Articles/The_evolving_distribution_and_role_of_press _releas_16269.aspx (accessed October 3, 2016).

2. Richard Sobel, "The High Cost of 'Free' Photo Voter Identification Cards," Charles Hamilton Houston Institute for Race & Justice at Harvard Law School, June 1, 2014, http://today.law.harvard.edu/wp- content/uploads/2014/06/FullReportVoterIDJune20141.pdf (accessed October 3, 2016).

3. U.S. Government Accountability Office, "Issues Related to State Voter Identification Laws," October 8, 2014, http://www.gao.gov/ products/GAO-14-634 (accessed December 19, 2016).

4. An editorial board memo is a memorandum to editorial board members or writers asking them to devote space to your issue or position.

5. Kevin Allen, "Journalists Still Think PR Pros Are Liars,"

Ragan's PR Daily, June 8, 2015, http://www.prdaily.com/Main/Articles/
Journalists_still_think_PR_pros_are_liars__18789.aspx (accessed
October 3, 2016).

6. Sophie Tatum, "Trump Surrogate Admits Falsifying Biographical
Claims," CNN.com, September 3, 2016, http://www.cnn.com/2016/09/
03/politics/mark-burns-donald-trump-interview/ (accessed on December
19, 2016).

7. Louis Nelson, "Trump Surrogate Mark Burns Lashes Out at
Media for Blackface Cartoon Fallout," POLITICO, September 1, 2016,
http://www.politico.com/story/2016/09/donald-trump-pastor-mark-
burns-blackface-cartoon-227657 (accessed December 19, 2016).

EIGHT

1. Jennifer Medina and Rob Davis, "After Dodging Harassment
Allegations, San Diego Mayor Is Reportedly Set to Resign," *New York
Times,* August 22, 2013, http://www.nytimes.com/2013/08/23/us/
harassment-suit-san-diego-mayor-bob-filner.html?_r=0 (accessed
December 19, 2016).

2. Kathleen Griffin, *The Forgiveness Formula: How to Let Go of Your
Pain and Move On with Life* (New York City: MJF Books, 2004), 142–143.

CONCLUSION

1. Arianna Huffington, *On Becoming Fearless: In Love, Work and Life*
(Boston: Little, Brown and Company, 2006), 95–96.

2. Olga Khazan, "Why Are There So Many Women in Public
Relations?" *Atlantic* (August 8, 2014).

3. Katty Kay and Claire Shipman, *The Confidence Code* (New York:
Harper Business, 2014), 158.

4. Jayson DeMers, "7 Things Good Communicators Always Do,"
Forbes, May 29, 2014, http://www.forbes.com/sites/jaysondemers/2014/
05/29/7-things-good-communicators-always-do/#766e6fa33dff (accessed
December 19, 2016).

5. Jeffrey J. Fox, *How to Become CEO: The Rules for Rising to the Top
of Any Organization* (New York: Hyperion, 1998), 134.

6. CareerCast, "The Most Stressful Jobs of 2015," (n.d.), http://www
.careercast.com/jobs-rated/most-stressful-jobs-2015 (accessed 2/9/17).

7. Rev. William J. Barber, interview with Bill Maher, *HBO Real Time
with Bill Maher,* Ep. 325, July 18, 2014.

INDEX

Abdullah, Khalil, 37
Advancement Project, x, 78
  communications campaigns, 6, 20
  core issues, 96
  litigation, 34–35, 73
  media conference calls, 6, 120
  persons involved with, 6, 22, 58, 73, 78, 90
  pitching stories and, 95, 96
  publications, 96, 113, 120
  school disciplinary policies and, 20–22, 25, 96, 120
  voting rights, barriers to voting, and, 5, 6, 34–35
Allen, Kevin, 117–118
Alpha Dog story(ies)
  challenging harmful, 10–11
  communicating your, 8–13
  overview, 9
Ambrogi, Drew, 45–46
American Legislative Exchange Council (ALEC), 4–5
Apologies, 130–132

Balogun, Jumoke, 142–143
Barber, William J., II, 47, 61–65, 77, 115, 143
  Forward Together Moral Movement and, 7, 65, 143

Moral Monday protests and, 7, 8, 64f, 77, 78, 115, 143, 153n4
North Carolina State Conference of the NAACP and, 76, 153n4
  overview, 47
Belin, Marty, 51–52, 52f, 78
Belton, Danielle, 80, 118
Bennett, Bo, 66
Big, thinking, 40–41
Big-picture thinking, 41, 61
Blogging, 85
Bold, being, 42–43
Brown, Les, 41
Burnout, preventing, 141
Burns, Mark, 119
Bush, George W., 124
Butland, Dale, 12, 17–18
Byers, Dylan, 33

Call/pitch lists, weekly
  developing, 106–109
  purpose of, 106
Card, Andrew, 124
Cave, Jeralyn, 71
CCRR framework, 86, 92, 94
Chan-Kent, Hilary, 118
Charlton, John, 87
Colburn, Bruce, xi
Coles, David, 37

Color of Change, 4, 5
Communications
    acknowledging all, 55–56
    for mission-driven organizations,
        2–8
    scope of the term, 1
    and your seat at the table, 13–15
Communications team integrated in
    strategic discussions, 13
Communicators, 13–14, 19
Confidence Code, The (Kay and
    Shipman), 138
Contacting the media, 28–34
Cooke, Jessica Thomas, 118
Creativity, xiv–xv, 36–38, 97, 105,
    113–114. *See also specific topics*
    in action, 46–52
    and challenging oneself to conceive,
        38–40
    in developing weekly call/pitch lists,
        108–109
    digital media and, 116–117
    and implementation, 43–46
    in organizing and facilitating
        engaging events, 124–125
    using two methods at the same time,
        50
Credibility, xiii–xiv, 17–19, 87,
    106–107, 114, 125, 129–131
    in action, 34–35
    being informed and, 28–34
    developing and using your network
        and, 103–105
    engaging editorial boards and,
        110–112
    keeping your word, 19–22
    and knowing what's newsworthy,
        23–28
    third-party validators and, 103, 104,
        118–121
    when pitching stories, 99–102
Cregor, Matt, 120
Crises, 126–127
Crisis communications, steps in
    step 1: avert a crisis before it begins,
        127–128

step 2: outline your goals and
    objectives, 129–130
step 3: tell the truth and apologize,
    130–132
step 4: beware of the drip…drip…
    drip, 133
step 5: seek professional help, 133–135
Crisis communications assistance,
    benefits for paying for, 134

DeMers, Jayson, 138
Denver Police Department, 20, 53, 68
Dianis, Judith Browne, 22, 67
Digital media
    maximizing, 115–117
    scope of the term, 116
    targeting both traditional media
        and, 50
Durbin, Richard "Dick," 67, 98, 105

Eaton, Rosanell, 64f, 144
Editorial board meetings, 109–110
    possible outcomes for, 109
Editorial boards, 109
    engaging, 109–110
Editorials. *See* Op-eds
Education Week, 21, 22
Eichner, James, 35
Embargoes, news/media, 19–20
Evangelism, xiii
    defined, xiii
    public relations and communications
        as, x
Events, engaging
    organizing and facilitating, 124–125
Executives, 14

Facebook, 83. *See also* Social media
Facebook Live, 83–84
Fear, using the four principles to lead
    in the midst of, 137–141
    feeding the spirit, 141–146
Fearlessness, 138
Ferrazzi, Keith, 41
Filner, Bob, 127–128
Follow-up, 57, 98

Foner, Mow, 43–44
Fonville, Phil, 115
Forgiveness, 132
Forward Together Moral Movement,
  7, 65, 143. *See also* Moral Monday
  protests
Fox, Jeffrey J., 43, 140

Glenn, John, 17
Goals and objectives, outlining,
  129–130
Goodell, Roger, 131, 133
Gordy, Cynthia, 6, 64
Greer, Alana, 105
Griffin, Kathleen, 132

Hair, Penda D., 73
Hamer, Fannie Lou, 27
Hettrick, Chelsea, 42–43
Hewitt, Damon, 120
Honesty, 130–132
Huffington, Arianna, 137–138

Implementation of ideas, 43–46
Influencers, targeting, 90
Infographics, 37
Information. *See also specific topics*
  creativity in methods of selecting
  and sharing, 37–38
  websites used to share, 50–51
Instagram, 84. *See also* Social media

Journalist associations, 34
Journalists, contacting, 28–34

Kawasaki, Guy, x
Kay, Katty, 138
Kerry, John F., 124
Kiley, Jamie, 71

Larabee, Michael, 70–72
Latvala, Jack, 6
Learning as much as possible, 56–57
Lesbian, gay, bisexual, transgender,
  and queer (LGBTQ) youth of color,
  142–143

LinkedIn, 84. *See also* Social media

Maher, Bill, 143
Mandela, Nelson, 40
Martinez, Pam, 53–54
Martinez-Johnson, Gebe, 69–70
McBride, Michael, 89
Media. *See also specific topics*
  collecting information on members
  of, 28–34
  creativity in breaking through to the,
  37–38
  targeting both traditional and digital,
  50
Media conference calls
  of Advancement Project, 6, 120
  organizing, 49, 139
Media embargoes, 19–20
Mesfin, Salem, 71
Milhiser, Ian, 78
Mission-driven organizations,
  communications for, 2–8
Mistakes, 132, 140
Moral Monday protests, 64f, 77–78,
  100
  arrests at, 51, 52f
  first rally, 51, 52f, 78, 143
  Marty Belin and, 51, 52f
  North Carolina (NC) NAACP and, 7,
  51, 64f, 115, 153n4
  origins, 76, 154n4
  photos, videos, and, 115
  Real Time with Bill Maher and, 143
  William Barber II and, 7, 8, 64f, 77,
  78, 115, 143, 153n4
Moral Movement, 47

National Association for the Advance-
  ment of Colored People (NAACP)
  Legal Defense and Education Fund
  (LDF), 120
  North Carolina (NC) chapter, 7, 51,
  63–65, 73, 76, 115, 153n4
Network, developing and using your,
  103–105
Never Eat Alone (Ferrazzi), 41

New York Times, 35, 41, 46–48, 101–102
News, reading
  with the intention of acting on what you've read, 48–49
News embargoes, 19–20
Newsome, Bree, 90
Newsworthy stories, knowing which stories are, 23–28
  questions to ask regarding capturing reporters' interest, 27
"No," hearing and responding to, xvi, 66, 69–75

Obama, Barack, xi–xii
On Becoming Fearless (Huffington), 137–138
O'Neil, Mary Evelyn Rider, 64f
Op-eds (guest columns), utilizing, 112–114

Packaging the story, 121–123
Palmer, Dian, xi
Palmer, Janay, 88, 130–131
Periscope, 83–84. *See also* Social media
Perseverance. *See* Relentlessness
Petition, organizing an online, 49
Pictures, utilizing, 51–52
Pitch lists. *See* Call/pitch lists
Pitching stories
  Advancement Project and, 95, 96
  proactively, 94–103
Plan, having a, 58–60
Police, 51, 52f, 63f
  in schools, 20, 25, 30–31, 53, 68f, 120
Police brutality, 26, 30, 89
Police shootings, 26, 89, 144
Press conferences. *See* Media conference call
Preston, Eric, 115
Prison. *See* School-to-prison pipeline
Professional help, seeking, 133–135
Public relations (PR), defined, 2
Public relations (PR) professional organizations and associations, 34

Public relations (PR) tactics, 93–94. *See also specific topics*
  recruiting and utilizing third-party validators, 117–122

Race Forward, 50–51
Racial disparities, 67, 142–143. *See also* Voting, barriers to
  in school discipline, 20, 36–37
Racial justice, 39, 107, 118, 142, 143. *See also* Advancement Project; Color of Change; National Association for the Advancement of Colored People; Race Forward
Regan, Dave, 11–13, 17
Rejection, xvi, 66, 69, 72. *See also* "No"
Relentlessness, xvi, 66–74, 122–123. *See also specific topics*
  in action, 78–81
  keep believing, 75–78
  knowing when to back off, 74–75
  in recruiting and utilizing third-party validators, 121
  on social media, 89–91
  when developing weekly call/pitch lists, 107–108
  when pitching stories, 97–99
  when using digital media, 117
Responsiveness, xv, 53–55, 135. *See also specific topics*
  in action, 61–65
  in apologizing, 131–132
  and averting crises, 128
  in dealing with problems, 133
  defined, xv
  on social media, 91–92
  when engaging editorial boards, 112
  when packaging the story, 123
  when pitching stories, 102–103
Restorative Justice, 36–37
Rice, Ray, 88, 130–131, 133
Rich, Motoko, 29
Robinson, Rashad, 4
Romney, Mitt, xii
Rosenblatt, Alan, 116–118

Rosenthal, Steve, 124

School disciplinary policies, Advancement Project and, 20–22, 25, 96, 120
School discipline, racial disparities in, 20, 36–37
School-to-prison pipeline, 22, 25, 31, 38, 54, 67, 78–80, 98, 104, 105
Schools
 police in, 20, 25, 30–31, 53, 68f, 120
 Restorative Justice in, 36–37
Schultz, Ed, 98
Scott, Keith Lamont, 89
Service Employees International Union (SEIU), x, xvi, 69
Service Employees International Union (SEIU) District 1199 (WV/KY/OH), x, xi, xvi, 3, 10, 17, 58
Sexual harassment, 127–128
Shah, Nirvi, 21–22
Shalhoub, Tony, xi
Shipman, Claire, 138
Sinocruz, Jason, 55
Snapchat, 84. *See also* Social media
Sobel, Richard, 107
Social media, 82–86
 the bottom line on, 92
 creative uses of, 88–89
 credibility on, 86–88
 relentlessness on, 89–91
 responsiveness on, 91–92
Spirit, feeding the, 141–146
St. George, Donna, 54, 66–69, 105
Stewart, Sally, 9–10
Storify, using, 50
Strickland, Ted, xi, 97
Surveying staff, 44–45

Tactics vs. principles, 15–16
Taxpayers Bill of Rights (TABOR), xi
Tenants and Workers United (TWU), 36, 71–72
Tetreault, Ann Louise, xi
Thinking, big-picture, 41, 61
Thinking big, 40–41

Third-party validators
 categories of, 118
 developing relationships with, 118–119, 121
 recruiting and utilizing, 117–122
Thomas, Eric (Hip Hop Preacher), 41
Thomas, Gregory, 120
Tibebu, Elizabeth, 71
Trump, Donald J., 119
Twitter, 84. *See also* Social media

Videos. *See also* Social media
 to share messages, 49
 utilizing, 51
Visuals, utilizing, 51–52
Voices of Youth in Chicago Education, 67f
Voting, barriers to, 37, 144
 anti-voting measures and voter suppression laws, 4, 6, 34–35, 65
 organizations that challenge, 5
 voter ID laws, 73, 74, 107, 108, 144
Voting rights
 activism and advocacy, 5, 6, 34–35, 65, 73–74, 96, 107, 108, 139
 in the media, 46–48, 74, 107, 108, 122
Voting Rights Act of 1965, Section 2 of, 34, 35

Washington Post, the, 21, 31, 66, 68, 70–72, 114, 139
Webinar, organizing a, 49
Websites
 used to share information, 50–51
Wegman, Jesse, 35, 47
Wenger, Victoria, 70
Wiedenkeller, Pat, 32
Williams, Becky, 18
Williams, Jesse, 90
Wilmot, Kiera, 24–26, 78–80, 105
Wilmot, Marie, 105
Winfrey, Oprah, 42
Wolf, Richard, 73–74

YouTube, promoting with, 49

ABOUT THE AUTHOR

 **JENNIFER R. FARMER** is a leading professional in communications strategy. She has made her mark in social justice movements for close to fifteen years, having held a range of senior leadership positions with racial justice, labor, and faith-based groups. She currently serves as communications director for PICO National Network and is the founder of Spotlight PR, LLC, whose mission is to develop and distribute high-impact public relations trainings for communicators.

Among her credits is work with the Rev. Dr. William J. Barber II, president of the North Carolina State Conference of the NAACP and architect of the Forward Together Moral

Movement. She led communications and outreach work in support of the weekly Moral Monday protests he organized beginning in April 2013. This included promoting the NC NAACP's legal challenge to North Carolina's 2013 restrictive voting measure, H.B. 589, which was overturned in July 2016.

Farmer's understanding of the intersection of policy, advocacy, and media has helped establish the groups she's worked with as leading voices in contemporary civil rights. She promoted the work of these organizations with news stories and TV segments in leading print, digital, and broadcast media outlets, including the *New York Times*, the *Wall Street Journal*, the *Washington Post*, *POLITICO*, Al Jazeera America, MSNBC, *Real Time with Bill Maher*, and *The Rachel Maddow Show*.

Farmer has a range of experiences spearheading national and state campaigns to affect social change. She's held positions in the public and nonprofit sectors, including roles with the Ohio Department of Transportation, the Ohio Senate Democratic Caucus and the Center for Progressive Leadership, where she trained and coached leaders seeking elected office.

She serves on the national advisory board for the National Center for State Courts' Community Engagement in the State Courts initiative, a project designed to promote racial and ethnic fairness in the courts. Farmer earned a Bachelor of Arts in English and Political Science from the University of Rochester. She is the proud mother of two and lives in northern Virginia.

Berrett–Koehler
Publishers

Berrett-Koehler is an independent publisher dedicated to an ambitious mission: *Connecting people and ideas to create a world that works for all.*

We believe that the solutions to the world's problems will come from all of us, working at all levels: in our organizations, in our society, and in our own lives. Our BK Business books help people make their organizations more humane, democratic, diverse, and effective (we don't think there's any contradiction there). Our BK Currents books offer pathways to creating a more just, equitable, and sustainable society. Our BK Life books help people create positive change in their lives and align their personal practices with their aspirations for a better world.

All of our books are designed to bring people seeking positive change together around the ideas that empower them to see and shape the world in a new way.

And we strive to practice what we preach. At the core of our approach is Stewardship, a deep sense of responsibility to administer the company for the benefit of all of our stakeholder groups including authors, customers, employees, investors, service providers, and the communities and environment around us. Everything we do is built around this and our other key values of quality, partnership, inclusion, and sustainability.

This is why we are both a B-Corporation and a California Benefit Corporation—a certification and a for-profit legal status that require us to adhere to the highest standards for corporate, social, and environmental performance.

We are grateful to our readers, authors, and other friends of the company who consider themselves to be part of the BK Community. We hope that you, too, will join us in our mission.

A BK Business Book

We hope you enjoy this BK Business book. BK Business books pioneer new leadership and management practices and socially responsible approaches to business. They are designed to provide you with groundbreaking and practical tools to transform your work and organizations while upholding the triple bottom line of people, planet, and profits. High-five!

To find out more, visit **www.bkconnection.com**.

Berrett–Koehler
Publishers

Connecting people and ideas
to create a world that works for all

Dear Reader,

Thank you for picking up this book and joining our worldwide community of Berrett-Koehler readers. We share ideas that bring positive change into people's lives, organizations, and society.

To welcome you, we'd like to offer you a free e-book. You can pick from among twelve of our bestselling books by entering the promotional code **BKP92E** here: http://www.bkconnection.com/welcome.

When you claim your free e-book, we'll also send you a copy of our e-newsletter, the *BK Communiqué*. Although you're free to unsubscribe, there are many benefits to sticking around. In every issue of our newsletter you'll find

- A free e-book
- Tips from famous authors
- Discounts on spotlight titles
- Hilarious insider publishing news
- A chance to win a prize for answering a riddle

Best of all, our readers tell us, "Your newsletter is the only one I actually read." So claim your gift today, and please stay in touch!

Sincerely,

Charlotte Ashlock
Steward of the BK Website

Questions? Comments? Contact me at bkcommunity@bkpub.com.

Certified
Corporation
bcorporation.net